To

Zack

CHRISTMAS 2015

Many happy and

large returns!

B Strud

Buy, Hold, and SELL!

Buy, Hold, and SELL!

The Investment Strategy That Could Save You from the Next Market Crash

Ken Moraif

WILEY

Cover design: Wiley

Published by John Wiley & Sons, Inc., Hoboken, New Jersey.
Published simultaneously in Canada.

For general information on our other products and services or for technical support, please contact our Customer Care Department within the United States at (800) 762-2974, outside the United States at (317) 572-3993 or fax (317) 572-4002.

Wiley publishes in a variety of print and electronic formats and by print-on-demand. Some material included with standard print versions of this book may not be included in e-books or in print-on-demand. If this book refers to media such as a CD or DVD that is not included in the version you purchased, you may download this material at http://booksupport.wiley.com. For more information about Wiley products, visit www.wiley.com.

Library of Congress Cataloging-in-Publication Data:
Moraif, Ken.
    Buy, hold, and sell! : the investment strategy that could save you from the next market crash / Ken Moraif.
       pages cm
    Includes index.
     ISBN 978-1-118-95149-1 (hardback); ISBN 978-1-118-95151-4 (epdf);
     ISBN 978-1-118-95150-7 (epub)
  1. Investments. 2. Retirement income–Planning. 3. Investment analysis. I. Title.
  HG4521.M837 2015
  332.6–dc23

                            2014036990

Printed in the United States of America

10 9 8 7 6 5 4 3 2 1

For my mom, who taught me how to save and invest,
and made me who I am today.

Contents

Acknowledgments

I want to thank:
Money Matters' beloved and most valued clients.
The astute, inquisitive, and engaged listeners of my radio show.

The patient, long-suffering, and dedicated Cindy Brown, who put up with all of my quirks and calendar issues.

My three wonderful daughters, who never hesitate to criticize me and keep me on the straight and narrow.

And always, my beautiful, talented, and supportive wife Fay.

Introduction

One Bear Market Can Change Your Life Forever

How would you feel if you lost over 78 percent of your retirement investments in one bad market?

I'd been doing a weekly radio show for four years when I was asked to speak at the "Managing Your Money" conference in Arlington, Texas. After my presentation to some 4,000 attendees, I walked offstage to find a man in his late fifties waiting for me. He said, "Ken, glad to meet you. I listen to your radio show every week."

"Thanks," I said, shaking his hand.

"Do you know how much money I had before this last bear market?"

This was 2002. The tech bubble had recently burst. I was afraid this was going to be a sad story. "No," I said, "how much did you have?"

"Three million dollars."

"Wow, that's great," I said. "Congratulations."

"Do you know much money I have now?"

I shook my head, bracing myself.

"I have $650,000."

I remember looking at the man. I couldn't believe he was standing, let alone smiling. "But tell me," I said, "To go from $3 million to $650,000, you had to see your investments drop to $2.5 million, then $2 million, then one and half... There were signposts along the way. Why didn't you get off the ride?"

And he said, "I had every intention. I planned to get out if my investments ever dropped down to two and a half million. But when they went down that far, I thought to myself, 'I'm down $500,000. I can't sell now. That'd be ridiculous.'"

I had the feeling I knew where he was going.

He continued: "So I drew a line in the sand: If my investments went down to $2 million, I'd sell for sure. But when they sank to that point, I did the same thing. I said to myself, 'Oh no, I'm down $1 million. I can't sell now, because the market will come back. I don't want to be the fool who sells at the bottom.'"

He went on. "Everybody was telling me that the market was going to bounce back. I didn't want to miss the rebound." He shook his head. "I never got out. I rode the market all the way to the bottom, and lost more than 70 percent of my money."

I wanted to say something encouraging to this poor guy, so I said, "I admire your ability to smile." I meant it.

"I could smile, or I could cry," he said. "I choose to smile."

The Inspiration behind This Book

I don't want you to end up like that former millionaire. I want you to smile because you're playing with your grandkids, perfecting your golf game, or dancing on the beach with your spouse. I don't want you to have to go through the pain of losing the retirement you've earned. You worked hard, and you've looked forward to this time in your life. I want it to be the best time in your life. I want your retirement to be like your second childhood without parental supervision.

I want your retirement to be your second childhood without parental supervision.

— *Ken Moraif*

And I want to help you get there. I want to convince you of the need to buy, hold, and *SELL*. In today's financial world, you face volatile markets, huge deficits, and even the risks of governments going bankrupt—all of which add up to the possibility of huge losses.

With those prospects, I think it's just plain irresponsible to simply ride the market. You need to have a proactive plan that includes a sell strategy.

But it's not easy. You've probably heard the same advice the unlucky investor followed. "The market will come back. Don't be the fool who sells at the bottom. You don't want to miss the rebound." It's popular advice. If you Google "investment advice," you'll probably find information that tells you to "hold forever" and "just diversify." I've worked as a financial advisor since 1988, and have heard these buy–hold myths propagated on the investing public over and over again. Sometimes I've heard them from people like the man in the story; investors who believed in the myths that later destroyed their retirement dreams.

In Part One of this book, we'll discuss the reasons why buy–hold is a bad idea. In Part Two, we'll debunk the myths that may keep you from being proactive. In Part Three, we'll explore the ways to use a sell strategy. And we'll have some fun doing it along the way, with the help of a few of my favorite TV characters.

By understanding that most buy–hold recommendations are indeed myths, you'll be able to stand your ground when necessary. You'll be able to execute your sell strategy with confidence. You won't be just another placid sheep that blindly follows the rest of the flock right off a cliff.

If you're retired or close to retirement, you cannot afford to be a sheep, or, to mix metaphors, to go along for the ride, allowing your investments to chauffeur you around. You have to be in the driver's seat. You have to be proactive, and very, very disciplined so that you can avoid the losses that could ruin your retirement. Remember the gentleman in our story? If he had stuck to his guns and said, "Okay, my investments are down to two and a half million. I'm out," he would have felt the pain of losing half a million dollars, but I suspect that was nothing compared to the way he felt when 78 percent of his money disappeared.

Protect your well-deserved retirement. Though nothing is certain in the world of finance, you can take action with your investments, and help avoid devastating losses. The first step? Read on, so that you can arm yourself with the knowledge that buy and hold is really just buy and hope, not a viable investment strategy—especially for anyone over 50.

Buy, Hold, and SELL!

Part One

THE TROUBLE WITH BUY-HOLD: WHY IT'S DANGEROUS TO YOUR FINANCIAL HEALTH

Chapter 1

Buy and Hold: A Bad Strategy for Anyone over 50?

I f you're over 50 and still investing the way you did when you were 35, you're in danger. You may be inadvertently putting yourself at risk of losing your hard-earned money, your desired lifestyle, and even your ability to retire.

You can't take the risks you did when you were younger. You're not in the game for growth anymore; you're in it to protect your principal. You need to protect it from taxes, from inflation, and from bear markets. When you get within five years of retirement, you need to shift your focus to protecting what you have built. It's easier said than done. All of a sudden you have to adopt a mindset that's 180 degrees from your former strategy. The buy-hold philosophy may have even helped you earn your wealth. It doesn't matter now. That strategy is no longer your friend, even if you're the best investor in the world.

3

Even the Best Investor . . .

Let's say you *are* the best investor in the history of the world. Over the past 30 years, you've made 20 percent every single year. You're a legend. They erected a 20-foot bronze statue of you on Wall Street. Every day, all the brokers and investors who pass by rub your foot for luck. You've amassed a huge estate—a phenomenal amount of money—and plan to retire in six months. Everything is great, except that it's now January 2008, and you believe in the buy-hold myth. What happens next? You lose half your money in that one year. Even if you end up with a lot of money after the crash, you now have a lifestyle half as nice as the one you were expecting. No matter how much money you have, if you've worked hard to ensure yourself a certain level of comfort, having to cut that dream in half is going to hurt.

© Randy Glasbergen
glasbergen.com

INVESTMENTS AND
RETIREMENT PLANNING

"Many people like to start a new hobby when they retire.
Hunting and gathering might be a good choice for you."

SOURCE: Randy Glasbergen.

You now also have the psychological pain of seeing your dreams and aspirations evaporate in front of your eyes. Should you retire after all? Maybe you should delay retirement? At this time in your life, you should not be experiencing this kind of anxiety, stress, or panic.

Buying into the Buy-Hold Myth

If buy-hold is such a dangerous strategy, why do people believe it? Because it seemed to work well for so long. Baby boomers, who account for 26 percent of the total U.S. population, were a large part of the workforce when they were younger. For many years, this 79-million-member generation was working in the labor market and building their retirement funds.

Did you notice what I said? People were *working* and *building* their retirement funds. When you were one of these working and investing people, you lived on the wages from your job while adding to your investment account. Your situation disguised what was really happening. For example, during one year you might have lost 20 percent of your investments, but since you were working, you also added to your account. At year-end, you didn't see a 20 percent loss reflected in your account; in fact, you may have had the same amount of money you had at the beginning of the year (see Figure 1.1). It would have been easy to think, "I didn't lose any money. Buy-hold worked."

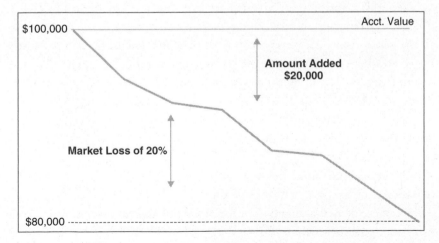

Figure 1.1   Added versus Lost

But you can see that it didn't. You broke even because you added to your investments. When you're still working, you're growing your money. You're putting money in your account. During bad times you're buying low. You're not as concerned about losses as you will be later in life. Being in the labor force muffles the actual experience of losing money.

The buy-hold strategy seems validated when you're working, but its problems are just disguised. When you retire, you'll see the real face of buy-hold. You'll be keenly aware of your losses. If you take out 5 percent for living expenses and then lose 20 percent of your investments in a bad market, you'll be down 25 percent at the end of the year. Your wages won't be there to cover your losses. You won't think you broke even. Worse than that, you'll have to change a few things in your life. You can't continue to live the way you did on just 75 percent of your former income. Look at it this way: Let's say you're still working, and one day your boss comes into your office. "Sorry," she says, "starting today we have to cut your pay 25 percent." What would you have to do? You'd have to rearrange your life dramatically to make up for your lost income.

> You can be young without money but you can't be old without it.   —Tennessee Williams, playwright

When you retire, your investments are your income. If you lose large quantities of money in a bear market and you are living on that money at the same time, your money probably won't last until you're eighty. Now, maybe you look forward to the day when you can run out of money, move back in with the kids, spend time with your grandchildren, and change diapers at three o'clock in the morning, but on the off-chance you have different ideas for retirement, you need to protect your money. The buy-hold strategy doesn't safeguard your money. It puts your investments at risk.

What do you think the chances are that we will have a bear market between now and the rest of your life?

I believe it is practically a certainty there will be another one, and buy-hold guarantees that you will take a loss when it comes.

Chapter 2

60 Is the New 40

What Does That Mean for Your Investments?

A while back, I was flying home from a financial planning conference, and the man sitting next to me on the plane was reading
a newspaper. I could tell something he was reading was really
bothering him. Curiosity eventually got the best of me, and I asked,
"Excuse me, but what is it that's bothering you so much?"

"Well, look what it says here," he said, showing me the paper's head-
line. "It says, 'Life expectancy to reach 120.'"

"So what's wrong with that?"

"What's wrong with that!?" he said. "Can you imagine your
90-year-old son moving back in with you? Oh my gosh, he still hasn't
gotten a job!"

How Long Will You Live?

A hundred and twenty years old may seem like a stretch, but the fact is that people are living a lot longer today than they ever did before. According to the Social Security Administration, males born in 2007 can expect to live to 75, while women born in the same year will live to 80 on average. Now, take a look at the chart in Figure 2.1.

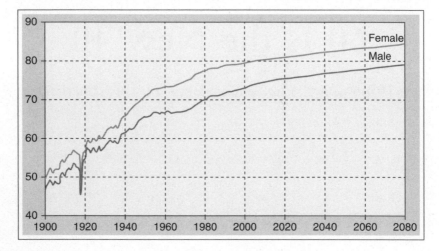

Figure 2.1 Social Security Population Projections, 1997

In 1900, neither men nor women were expected to live past 50 years old! In a little more than one century, we've gained 25 years or more.

It gets more interesting. Most life expectancy charts look at how long you'll live from birth, but there are also statistics on how long you'll live if you're older. In 1950, a 65-year-old was expected to live to be 77 years old. By 2009, it was estimated that a 65-year-old would live to see 84. Think about it; in 1950 the average 65-year-old would live 12 more years. The average 65-year-old today will live nearly 20 years. That's a substantial difference.

Remember, these are averages. You could live longer. Life expectancies are determined by averages. For example, researchers look at a thousand 65-year-olds, and when they find the age where 500 are living and 500 are dead, that's the crossover point—the life expectancy. If you're still alive at that age, you're in the 50th percentile. But what if you take especially good care of yourself or have really good genes? You'd likely be in a higher percentile, and could live years longer.

Over the next few years it is very likely that scientists and doctors will develop cures for the main killers we face today. It looks more and more like cancer and heart disease will suffer the fate of diseases like polio and tuberculosis. Good riddance! When these advances are made, life expectancy will rise again. It's highly possible that you will live more years in retirement than the number of years you worked to accumulate the money that you will retire on!

What Does a Long Life Mean for Retirement?

Living longer means you'll have more time to enjoy retirement, right? More time to golf, play with the grandkids, just enjoy life. Unless it means you have to delay retirement, to work longer in order to make sure you have enough money to live out those extra years.

In 1995, Gallup consultants found that most Americans expected to retire at 60. But now, according to a 2011 Gallup poll, only 28 percent plan to retire before they're 65.

© Randy Glasbergen
www.glasbergen.com

INVESTMENTS AND
RETIREMENT PLANNING

GLASBERGEN

"If you work hard and invest wisely, you can
afford to turn 65 on your 80th birthday."

SOURCE: Randy Glasbergen.

When I was young I thought that money was the most important thing in life; now that I am old I know that it is.

—Oscar Wilde, writer and poet

There could be a few reasons behind this trend. People born in 1937 or prior to that year could claim full Social Security benefits at age 65. People born after that have to wait until 66 or 67. That might be one reason. The Society of Actuaries reports that people are nervous about inflation's effect on their retirement—that could be another reason. Yet another reason might be that the majority of workers don't receive pensions anymore. Since most companies have shifted from providing defined-benefit pension plans to offering defined contribution plans, the average worker is now in charge of investing his retirement money. Will those investments generate enough income for the number of years that people are now expected to live? All of those concerns certainly contribute to the delayed retirement phenomena, but I don't think any of them are the main reason behind the shift.

The 2011 Gallup poll found that for the first time ever, more Americans were afraid of outliving their savings than were comfortable with their ability to retire. More than half of workers between the ages of 50 and 64 feared they wouldn't be able to maintain their current standard of living once they retired.

They may be right to be scared. In October 2008, the Congressional Budget Office reported that Americans had lost roughly $2 trillion in retirement savings over 15 months.

I think that's probably the biggest reason behind American's fear of running out of money. They lost their shirts in 2008. Losing half your money in just one year will make you very nervous about the future.

The Longevity–Retirement–Investment Equation

I want to help you avoid the pitfalls that claimed those retirement dollars in 2008. I want you to live long and prosper. In order to do that, I think it's important you understand the longevity–retirement–investment equation.

> Live long and prosper.
> —Mr. Spock, first officer, USS *Enterprise*

If you retired back in 1950 at the age of 65, you could expect to live another 12 years. If you were only going to live 12 years, you wouldn't worry so much about taxes, inflation, and bear markets. Sure, you wouldn't want to experience them, but at the same time you could pretty much put all of your money in a box in the backyard, take out what you need to live on every month, and it would most likely last 12 years.

But in today's world, you've got to make your money last for 19 years or more. You *do* have to worry about inflation, taxes, and bear markets. And you have to recognize that longevity is one of the biggest enemies to your financial well-being. If you live a long time, your money has to last a lot longer. If you live into your 90s, the more heavy lifting your investments need to do to support your lifestyle. You're asking a lot more from your money.

The longer you live, the more likely you are to have health-care costs, too (see Figure 2.2). It doesn't matter how well you take care of

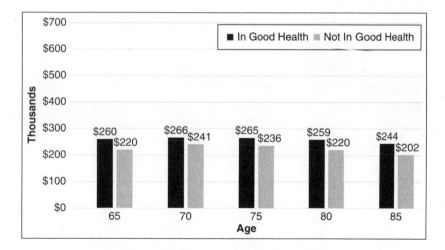

Figure 2.2 Mean Remaining Lifetime Health-Care Costs by Age and Health Status, 2009 Dollars

Note: Costs are for households turning 65 in 2009. Increases in medical costs are projected to place subsequent birth cohorts at greater risk.

Source: "Does Staying Healthy Reduce Your Lifetime Health Care Costs?" Center for Retirement Research, Boston College. Calculations based on the model described in Webb and Zhivan (2010b). © 2010, by Trustees of Boston College, Center for Retirement Research. All rights reserved.

yourself, it's just the price of longevity. In fact, the Center for Retirement Research at Boston College found that people who are healthy and live a long life spend more on health care than unhealthy people who die younger. Maintenance is more costly than junking the car.

Medicare does cover most issues, but not all. What if you need long-term care? Long-term care is not medical care, it is help with the "activities of daily living"—the everyday tasks that are just a part of life. Bathing yourself, driving yourself around, feeding yourself; these are the kinds of things that are considered activities of daily living. And though you may need assistance with those tasks, you don't need a doctor, so your medical insurance typically won't pay for the help you need. Neither will Medicare. It's even noted on Medicare.gov: "Medicare generally doesn't pay for long-term care."

"If you start drinking, smoking, and eating fatty food, you'll have enough retirement money to last the rest of your life."

SOURCE: Randy Glasbergen.

Depending on the need and duration of care, expenses can be enormous—up to $90,000 per year for dementia care in a skilled nursing facility (private room). And long-term care costs are rising. A recent MetLife Mature Market Institute survey found that long-term care provider costs rose far faster than the rate of inflation.

Imagine having to spend an additional $7,500 per month on health care on top of your normal expenses. Then imagine that the market goes down at the same time. You could be in a very dangerous situation. You could run out of money very quickly. How likely is this scenario? Over half of us will require some sort of long-term care during our lives, whether we need support for a few weeks after a surgery or years of care due to a serious illness.

Add to that the possibility of a bear market. I believe there is a 100 percent chance of a future bear market, but since I can't predict the future, we'll say there's a 90 percent chance. In the average bear market, the DOW goes down about 37 percent. In this (very likely) scenario, there's a 90 percent chance of a bear market with an average loss of 37 percent in your future. That's bad enough, but you may see more than one bear market. Over the past 100 years, we've had 33 bear markets. On average, that's one every three years.

Let's go back to you: If you had parents who lived into their 90s, or you eat well, or you take good care of yourself, you may live 30 years in your retirement. You could have 10 more bear markets in your life. Do the math. If you're taking money out of your investments while living through 10 bear markets, how long do you think your money is going to last?

But let's say you live a long time *and* are lucky. You stay active and healthy. You retire with over $1 million in investments. The economy is great, the market is strong, and you don't have to live through 10 bear markets to experience hardship—it could take only one. If you lose a third of your money in that one bad market, it can change your life forever. And that's just what happened to one unwary couple...

Chapter 3

The Bear and
the Lake House

Several years ago, a couple came into my firm to take advantage of the free consultation we offer. They sat down with us and explained their financial situation. They were retired, had $866,000 in investments, and were drawing $60,000 a year from those investments to cover their cost of living. "Wait a minute," we said, "You're taking out $60,000 a year? That's 7.5 percent. That's very, very high. Your investments cannot support that. It won't be very long before you run out of money."

"Yes, but here's what you don't understand," said the husband. "We retired in 2007 with one and a half million dollars. At that time $60,000 was 4 percent of our investments and we could handle it. The problem is that 2008 came along, and we lost nearly half our investments. Now we have $866,000, and even though the market went down, our expenses didn't, so we're spending the same amount."

Thinking they were all set for retirement, this couple had sold their existing home and bought a beautiful $750,000 lakefront home. They put the $300,000 they received from the sale of their house into the new house and wound up with a $450,000 mortgage. Every month they had a $2,700 mortgage payment.

"We know you're not clients yet," we said, "but after analysis, we have to tell you that you can't afford that house. You're going to have to sell it. You can take the equity you have in the house and buy a new house. Your house will be paid for. That will reduce your expenses by $2,700, and then you should be okay."

"But this is where the family congregates," said the wife. "The kids and the grandkids come all year round. They come for Christmas, for Thanksgiving, for birthdays. It's become the family home."

"We understand, but you can't afford it anymore. You've got two choices: You can sell this house, buy a new one, and afford to eat steak; or you can stay in this house and eat Beanie Weenies."

The wife thought about it for a moment. With tears in her eyes, she said, "For now, we'll eat Beanie Weenies."

They finally did put their lake house up for sale. They got to the point where they could no longer afford to stay in it. Unfortunately, by then it was 2009. Prices had fallen so low that they were going to have to sell it at a huge loss. Not only that, but the prospects of selling the house were bleak. A severe drought had caused the lake to recede a hundred and fifty feet. They no longer had lakefront property.

This couple worked hard and earned their retirement. Then, in *one year*, they saw their investments drop from $1.5 million to $866,000. Their problems snowballed from there. These folks were unprepared when the market tanked. They didn't have a defensive plan. One bear market changed their lives.

I don't mean to scare you, but I do want you to recognize the good, the bad, and the ugly when it comes to investing at this time of your life. I want you to be prepared for bear markets. I want you to protect your investments. I want your money to last as long as you do.

It's important that you understand that the game has changed. You're not only moving from offense to defense, but if you've recently retired, or are planning to retire, you're in the most important period of your investing life, and you need to make these years count.

I want your money to last as long as you do.
    —Ken Moraif

Chapter 4

The 10 Most Important Years of Your Investing Life

I f you had a choice, would you rather lose a third of your money when you're 60 years old or 75? Now don't worry. I know you don't want to lose your money at any time. I've written this book in order to help you avoid losses, but stay with me for a minute. If you *had* to lose a big chunk of change, do you think you'd be better off losing it when you first retired or 15 years later?

I suspect many of you will lean toward losing it right away instead of later. You think, "Wow, it'd be really scary to lose a third of my investments when I'm 75. I might have medical bills, and it would certainly be hard for me to go back to work." All true. It would be scary, and you would have a hard time recouping your losses. But in terms of your investments, you've made the wrong choice.

More Heavy Lifting

If you lose a third of your money when you're 75, it's still possible you could live the rest of your years on the remaining two-thirds of your investments and be just fine. To put it a bit bluntly, the older you get, the less work your money has to do because your life expectancy isn't that long.

The younger you are, the longer your life expectancy. Your money has to do more heavy lifting, because it needs to carry you for the rest of your life.

That's a serious issue, but it's not the only problem with losing money early in your retirement. You invest with the idea that you'll make money over time. If you lose a third of your money when you're 60, you haven't just lost that money, you've lost its time value. You'll miss out on all the income your money could have generated and all the potential gains you might have had in the next 15 to 20 years. That's a substantial amount of cash.

The Eighth Wonder of the World?

Albert Einstein is reputed to have said that compound interest is the eighth wonder of the world. And it's true—compound interest is amazing. You know how it works: You invest a sum of money, earn interest, and then reinvest the interest earned back into your original investment. Let's say you invest a million dollars (that's my favorite number—you'll notice I use it a lot), and you earn 5 percent interest yearly on that initial investment. After your first year, you'll have earned $50,000, so your new principal is $1,050,000. Now you invest all that money and earn 5 percent. By the end of the second year (assuming 5 percent interest), you'll have $1,102,500. If you continue to reinvest the interest you've earned, by year five you'll have $1,276,281. After 10 years, you'll have $1,628,894, and after 20 years you'll have $2,653,297. Even though you earned just 5 percent interest, you more than doubled your money in 20 years! See why compound interest feels like the eighth wonder of the world?

Reverse Compounding

If you lose money up front, you have lost all potential for compound interest, for growth going forward on that money. I've dubbed this negative process "reverse compounding." It works on the same time-dependent principals as compound interest, but has the opposite effect. This concept is easiest to explain by looking at the math, so I've created a couple of charts for you: Tables 4.1 and 4.2. Both of these charts assume that you retire with a million dollars, that you get a return of 5 percent each year, and that you take out 4 percent of your investments in the first year for living expenses. These examples also assume that your living expenses grow by 3.5 percent each year after the first year due to inflation, and that at one point during your retirement you experience a bear market.

Table 4.1   Losing 37 Percent in Year 15

Year of Retirement	Balance at Beginning of Year	Investment Gain/Loss for the Year	Withdrawal for Cost of Living	Total Gain/Loss	Balance at End of Year
1	1,000,000	50,000	40,000	10,000	1,010,000
2	1,010,000	50,500	41,400	9,100	1,019,100
3	1,019,100	50,955	42,849	8,106	1,027,206
4	1,027,206	51,360	44,349	7,012	1,034,218
5	1,034,218	51,711	45,901	5,810	1,040,028
6	1,040,028	52,001	47,507	4,494	1,044,521
7	1,044,521	52,226	49,170	3,056	1,047,577
8	1,047,577	52,379	50,891	1,488	1,049,065
9	1,049,065	52,453	52,672	(219)	1,048,846
10	1,048,846	52,442	54,516	(2,074)	1,046,772
11	1,046,772	52,339	56,424	(4,085)	1,042,687
12	1,042,687	52,134	58,399	(6,264)	1,036,423
13	1,036,423	51,821	60,443	(8,622)	1,027,801
14	1,027,801	51,390	62,558	(11,168)	1,016,633
15	1,016,633	(376,154)	64,748	(440,902)	575,731
16	575,731	28,787	67,014	(38,227)	537,503
17	537,503	26,875	69,359	(42,484)	495,019
18	495,019	24,751	71,787	(47,036)	447,983

Table 4.1 illustrates what happens when a bear market occurs 15 years into your retirement. The average bear market incurs a loss of 37 percent, so we'll assume that was your loss (by the way, bear markets can cost you even more—in 2008, you could have lost up to 57 percent). In this example, even though your investments took a bad hit, you can see that at the end of your 18th year, you still have $447,983.

But look at Table 4.2 to see what happens if you get hit with a bear market right off the bat.

Table 4.2   Losing 37 Percent in the First Year

Year of Retirement	Balance at Beginning of Year	Investment Gain/Loss for the Year	Withdrawal for Cost of Living	Total Gain/Loss	Balance at End of Year
1	1,000,000	**(370,000)**	40,000	(410,000)	590,000
2	590,000	29,500	41,400	(11,900)	578,100
3	578,100	28,905	42,849	(13,944)	564,156
4	564,156	28 208	44,349	(16,141)	548,015
5	548,015	27,401	45,901	(18,500)	529,515
6	529,515	26,476	47,507	(21,032)	508,483
7	508,483	25,424	49,170	(23,746)	484,737
8	484,737	24,237	50,891	(26,654)	458,083
9	458,083	22,904	52,672	(29,768)	428,315
10	428,315	21,416	54,516	(33,100)	395,214
11	395,214	19,761	56,424	(36,663)	358,551
12	358,551	17,928	58,399	(40,471)	318,080
13	318,080	15,904	60,443	(44,539)	273,541
14	273, 541	13,677	62,558	(48 881)	224,660
15	224,660	11,233	64,748	(53,515)	171,145
16	171,145	8,577	67,014	(58,547)	112,689
17	112,689	5,634	69,359	(63,725)	48,964
18	48,964	2,448	71,787	(69,339)	—

You run out of money in 18 years! You can see why it is so important to protect your money from large losses, especially in the early years.

The Most Important Years of Your Investing Life

I want you to have money when you're old. In order to have—and keep—your money, you need to understand this fact: the five years before you retire and the five years after you retire are the most important years of your entire financial life. As you can see from the examples I provided, if you lose mass quantities of your money during those years, you severely impair, if not completely destroy, your money's ability to support the lifestyle you want.

But why these particular 10 years? You can probably see why the five years before you retire are important. If you suddenly lose a fourth or half of your investments, you'll have two choices: retire later than you'd planned, or live a different retirement lifestyle.

> *I want you to have money when you are old.*
> *—Ken Moraif*

If you experience a big loss during the first five years *after* your retirement, you're faced with even more difficult choices: either change your lifestyle dramatically, or go back to work. The second choice could be a problem. Your skills may have atrophied. Your old company may have hired somebody else for your position. You'd probably have to compete against younger people. It can become very difficult to replace the income you've now lost.

Though the examples I've provided are hypothetical, the chance of a bear market in your lifetime is not. They tend to occur every three years, remember? You *could* lose a substantial amount of your retirement if you hold on to your investments during a bear market.

When you were young, you might have been able to recoup from a big loss. Once you're over 50, you're in a different game. You need to preserve as much of your net worth as you can. You need a different strategy, one that mitigates the downside of longevity and helps you withstand bear markets. You need to break free of the buy-hold mindset, or you might end up like the unlucky lady described in the next chapter.

Chapter 5

A Buy-Hold
Disaster Story

M iss Kitty worked hard her whole life, saved her money, and invested wisely. After selling the Long Branch Saloon in 2000, she retired with a million dollars in investments—a nice amount of money.

Kitty intended to enjoy retirement, travel a bit, maybe take a cruise with her beau Matt once a year. She would be careful, taking out just the prescribed 4 percent for living expenses, which in her case was $40,000. She planned her post-retirement lifestyle based on having this money available to her. With $1 million, she figured she was all set. And she might have been, if she hadn't believed the buy-hold myth.

In 2000, the first year of her retirement, Miss Kitty withdrew $40,000 as planned. Unfortunately, the market also took a chunk of her money. The S&P 500 lost 10.4 percent. Miss Kitty took out $40,000 and the market took out $101,400, leaving her with $858,600. Not a very good start to her retirement. (See Table 5.1.).

"Maybe you should think about protecting some of that money," suggested Matt.

"I'm not worried," said Kitty. "They say the market always comes back."

By 2001, Miss Kitty had $858,600 in investments, rather than a million. Her living expenses rose by 3.5 percent due to inflation, so she needed to take out $41,400, which is not 4 but 5 percent of $858,600. And again, she wasn't the only one taking money out of her account. The market took out 13.04 percent that year, costing Kitty $111,961. Her account balance shrank to $705,239.

The worst year of the tech bubble bear market was 2002. The market went down 23.37 percent. Miss Kitty lost $164,814 (23.37 percent of $705,239) and took out $42,849 for living expenses (the higher amount again due to inflation). Her investments were now less than $500,000. In three years, Miss Kitty lost half her money. Her retirement was not working out the way she planned. A cruise seemed like an extravagance, and she was so nervous about her finances that she was reluctant to get out of Dodge, even for a short trip. But Miss Kitty still believed in the buy-hold myth, so she stayed in the market.

And lo and behold, the market did come back. Though Kitty's living expenses continued to climb because of inflation, the bull market grew her investments. At the end of five years (near the end of 2007), Kitty's account balance was up to $558,533.

"Buy-hold does work," she said to Matt. "My investment value increased even though I took out all that money."

"Still seems dangerous to me to have all that money in the market right now," said Matt.

"You think everything's dangerous."

"That's why I'm still alive," said Matt.

Miss Kitty just waved him off. She was pretty happy, even though $558,533 was way less than the million she'd started with.

But 2008 came along. Remember that year? Miss Kitty certainly does. In 2008, the market took a dramatic dive. It dropped 38.49 percent, costing Kitty $214,979. Continued inflation meant that she needed to withdraw $52,672 for living expenses. By the end of 2008, Miss Kitty had just $290,881, less than a third of her original million dollars.

Inflation continued to increase by 3.5 percent each year. By 2009, Miss Kitty needed to take out $54,516 for expenses. That's 19 percent of $290,881 — *19 percent.*

Table 5.1   Miss Kitty's Buy-Hold Disaster

Year	Beginning Nest Egg	Amount Withdrawn	Market Return	Market Loss/Gain	Ending Nest Egg	Draw %
2000	1,000,000	40,000	−10.14	−101,400	858,600	4%
2001	858,600	41,400	−13.04	−111,961	705,239	5%
2002	705,239	42,849	−23.37	−164,814	497,575	6%
2003	497,575	44,349	26.38	131,260	584,487	9%
2004	584,487	45,901	8.99	52,545	591,131	8%
2005	591,131	47,507	3.00	17,734	561,358	8%
2006	561,358	49,170	13.62	76,457	588,645	9%
2007	588,645	50,891	3.53	20,779	558,533	9%
2008	558,533	52,672	−38.49	−214,979	290,881	9%
2009	290,881	54,516	23.45	68,212	304,577	19%
2010	304,577	56,424	12.78	38,925	287,078	19%

SOURCE: S&P 500.

"Seems like you're eating your seed corn," said Matt. "If you keep doing that, you won't have anything to plant come growing season."

"Oh, be quiet," said Miss Kitty. "I'm trying to think."

Miss Kitty knew she was in trouble. If her expenses kept going up while she was drawing on her investments, her money would continue to shrink at a rapid pace. Her investments would need to make 19 percent or more every single year for the rest of her life. And what if she got hit with another 38 percent or 23 percent loss?

"Do you think I can find an investment that will guarantee at least 19 percent for life?" she asked Matt, pretty sure she already knew the answer.

Matt shook his head.

"Do you see any way I can live a bit cheaper?" Miss Kitty thought she lived pretty frugally, but hoped that Matt might think of a way to cut costs.

But he shook his head again.

"Well then," said Miss Kitty with a sigh, "Guess I'll see if the saloon could use an old hand."

Miss Kitty had $1 million in investments, but 10 years after retirement, she had to go back to work (and by the way, Miss Kitty's story didn't include taxes and fees, which would have made the picture even bleaker). I ask you, dear readers, does this look like a happy ending to you? Do you want to have to find a job when you're 75? Or change your lifestyle drastically? Maybe have your kids support you?

I don't think so.

I think you want a comfortable retirement, one where you can play golf and take the occasional cruise without worrying about your finances. I don't believe the buy-hold strategy will get you there. In fact, I think it's a recipe for disaster. I think it's financial insanity, unless you want to end up like Miss Kitty.

Chapter 6

You Know You're a Buy-Holder If...

Wondering whether the buy-hold philosophy has a hold on you? Take this quiz and find out!

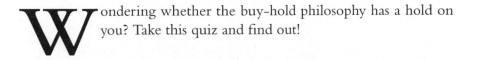

You know you're a buy-holder if:

_____ You think the market will always come back—and it's okay to lose 20–30 percent while you're waiting.

_____ Your spouse told you to sell in 2008, but you ignored your spouse because you knew better.

_____ You bought a diversified portfolio four years ago and have never looked at it since.

_____ Every instinct in your body is telling you to sell and you ignore each and every one.

_____ You still own the first investment you ever made.

_____ You're really good at buying but really lousy at selling.

_____ Losing a quarter of your money in the next bear market is okay with you.

_____ You think that taking money out of your declining portfolio is a recipe for financial security.

Chapter 7

Why Does Buy-Hold Even Exist?

My secretary Gail made a mean meatloaf from a recipe that had been in her family for generations. She passed the recipe on to her daughter, who made the dish the traditional way, too. One evening, when Gail's daughter was preparing meatloaf for a family dinner, she carefully discarded the ends of the meatloaf as she'd been taught. As she did so, she said, "Mom, I know I should slice off the ends of the meatloaf, but why?"

Gail stared at her. "You know, I'm not sure. My mom just always served it that way. She'll be here in a few minutes. Let's ask her." When her mother arrived, Gail and her daughter were anxious to solve the mystery of the meatloaf. "Why did I cut off the ends of the meatloaf?" said Gail's mom. "Easy. My serving tray was shorter than my baking pan. The meatloaf didn't fit unless I sliced off the ends."

Generational Amnesia

Gail had fallen into that old trap: "We do it that way because that's how we've always done it." The meatloaf mystery is a great example of generational amnesia—a big part of the buy-hold backstory.

Prior to the bear market of 2000, the market had gone up for nearly 20 years almost uninterrupted. Twenty years—that's basically an entire generation of investors. Figure 7.1 is what the market looked like during the time this lucky generation was investing, from 1981 through the end of 2000.

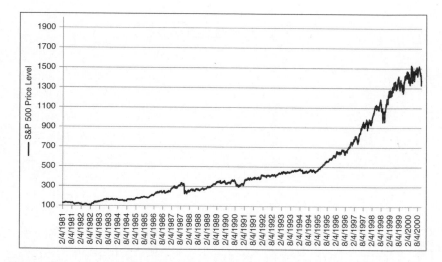

Figure 7.1   The 20-Year Bull Market (February 1981 to August 2000)

Look at the long gentle rise. It's a beautiful thing, isn't it? Why wouldn't you want to buy-hold? That long-running bull market never dipped too far down, and yes, it always came back. Add to that the fact that baby boomer investors were still working and contributing to their retirement plans and savings accounts, and they didn't need to live on their investments. Those three things combined validated buy-hold for 20 years.

During an entire generation's financial childhood, buy-hold worked. Boomers had no reason to question the strategy.

The Rest of the Story

But that beautiful 20-year bull market didn't last (see Figure 7.2). As Paul Harvey used to say, "And now, the rest of the story . . . "

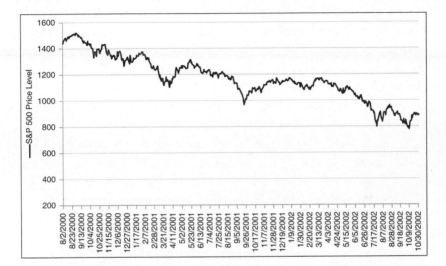

Figure 7.2   The 20-Year Bull Market Aftermath (August 2000 to October 2002).

Not only did that bull market not last, we haven't seen a nice upward slope like the one shown in Figure 7.1 in some time. The volatility that we've experienced recently may be bumpier than normal, but it's actually more typical than that smooth period from 1981–2000. It was an anomalous period in the history of the market. But that's when many of today's investors were introduced to the market, and that's when buy-hold caught on.

> In economics, things take longer to happen than you think they will, and then they happen faster than you thought they could.
> —Rudi Dornbusch, economist

The Rise of Mutual Funds

The mutual fund industry also grew during this glorious bull market, adding weight to the buy-hold myth. Don't get me wrong; I think mutual funds are a great invention that helped democratize investing. Before the advent of mutual funds, people who wanted to properly diversify and avail themselves of the latest research and access the best quality managers could do so only if they had millions of dollars to invest. The idea behind mutual funds was to pool all the investors' money so there would be enough dollars in that fund to hire the good managers and access the research and follow healthy investment strategies formerly available to only the very wealthy.

As you can see, mutual funds are terrific for the small investor. During that great bull market they really exploded, and are now the most popular form of investment for the average investor.

However, there's a built-in conflict: mutual fund companies make less money when people are out of the market. Because of this, mutual fund managers often encourage people to stay the course and stay in the market. The industry spends millions of dollars selling the idea that people should hold onto their investments no matter what, so that investors hear the buy-hold message over and over again from multiple media outlets.

And of course, buy-hold happened to work during that beautiful 20-year period of steady growth. The fact that it was working, and that the mutual fund industry kept promoting the idea made buy-hold *the* way to invest. And as with any idea, when it's repeated often enough, it becomes a powerful "truth."

The Best Coin-Flipper in the World

Once upon a time in a faraway land, coin flipping was hot. In fact, the biggest reality show on TV was *Heads or Tails?* Every week, everyone across the nation would tune in to see which coin flipper would win. At the beginning of the season, 1,000 participants tossed their coins in the air and called heads or tails. That first week, half the contestants were wrong, so there were only 500 on the show the next week. Half of those remaining contestants called their flips incorrectly, so the next week's episode featured only 250. On and on it went. Everyone had their favorite flipper, and would watch each week to cheer on their champion. Finally, after a tense contest between the last two contestants, one person called his flip correctly and was declared the winner. By that time, he had predicted heads or tails correctly 10 times in a row.

The entire nation—millions of viewers—thought the winner must have some extraordinary skill to call the flip correctly every time. The *Heads or Tails?* winner, because of his success, also believed in his own prowess. He was so sure of his remarkable abilities that he went on tour, explaining to all of his adoring fans where to put the coin on their hands, how to use the right amount of pressure in the flip, and how to take the room temperature into account. Everyone listened to this extremely skilled person. After all, he called the flip 10 times in a row; of course he knew what he was doing. Right?

That 19-year period from 1981 to 2000 enabled buy-holders to be expert coin flippers. Everyone (including themselves) thought they were geniuses, when in reality they were lucky. They happened to be the ones who tossed the coin 10 times in a row and called the flips correctly, but it wasn't talent: It was a rising tide that lifted all boats.

> It ain't the things that people don't know that's the problem. It's the things they do know that just ain't so.
>
> —Will Rogers, humorist

Unfortunately, now they believe in their prowess. I recently saw an interview where John Bogle, the founder and retired CEO of the Vanguard Group, said he thinks there will be two major 50 percent bear markets in the next decade. He basically said that's why you should buy and hold, because when the decade is over, you should have more money than at the beginning of the decade. What he believes can be true: for example, your portfolio was higher in 2013 than it was in 2000 if you had bought and held. But would you really want to suffer through the bear markets of 2000 and 2008 just to have slightly more money than you started with? And would that be a good reason to endure two more

50 percent bear markets over the next 10 years? In my view, that makes no sense. After all, there is no guarantee that the market will come back. Betting your retirement on the hope that the market will recover all of its losses during your lifetime is not a good financial plan, as we will discuss later on.

And is it any coincidence that Bogle, the mutual fund king, is a firm believer in buy-hold? Could Bogle be drinking his own Kool-Aid? Buy-hold worked for the mutual funds because they were in the right place at the right time during a long-run bull market. We can't rely on that.

The Famous Scene in *The Deer Hunter*

If you ever watched *The Deer Hunter*, you probably remember the Russian roulette scene. Robert DeNiro and Christopher Walken played two POWs who were forced by their Vietcong captors to play the deadly game. I recently read a discussion of the scene that included the answer to the question: How long could someone survive playing Russian roulette?

Traditional Russian Roulette is played with a single bullet in a six-shooter revolver. Someone spins the cylinder and slaps it closed. The player puts the gun to his head and pulls the trigger. He has a one-in-six chance of shooting himself, which means that mathematically, he'd live to tell the story about 83 percent of the time. Not bad odds, if the stakes weren't so high.

But the more often he plays the game, the more the odds work against him. In fact, if the game were played 100 times, the odds are that he would encounter a live bullet (and death) 17 times.

You may remember that in the film, DeNiro's character insisted on playing with three bullets in the chamber as part of a desperate escape plan. He raised the odds of dying to 50/50 for the first player. Both he and Walken survived. Their luck lasted long enough that they didn't kill themselves. That's the kind of luck this last generation had when they invested. But that kind of luck doesn't last. The odds get worse the longer the game is played. The longer you buy-hold, the greater the odds are that you will be exposed to large losses in a major bear market.

Chapter 8

What Do Economists Say about Buy-Hold?

S uppose I asked you to predict the weather tomorrow. Then I asked you to forecast the weather a year from now. Which prediction is more likely to be wrong (i.e., the riskier prediction)? The stock market is just the same: The longer the time horizon, the more chance you take that something in the future will come along and blow a big hole in your investments.

In 2012, Lubos Pastor of the University of Chicago Booth School of Business and Robert Stambaugh of the Wharton School at the University of Pennsylvania won the first Whitebox prize—awarded to outstanding financial research—for their paper on the volatility of stocks. After studying over 200 years of stock-market data, the professors found the longer an investor holds on to stocks, the more that volatility (and risk) increases. Over one year, stocks showed 17 percent annual volatility; over 30 years, 21 percent; and over 50 years, 23 percent. In an interview with Cheryl Casone of *Fox Business News*, Lubos said, "Investors looking into the future don't only buy the historical estimates, but also buy the uncertainty associated with those estimates, and the uncertainty compounds with time."

Pastor also noted the good fortune we boomers had during our prime investing years, saying, "The average historical return in the 20th century includes good luck, and it's not clear we'll have the same productivity growth in the future."

> *The average historical return in the 20th century includes good luck, and it's not clear we'll have the same productivity growth in the future.*
> —*Lubos Pastor*

Wharton professor Jeremy Siegel also considered long-term historical data when researching his classic investing book, *Stocks for the Long Run*. In his book, Siegel examined the financial market data from 1802 on, and argued that his research showed that investors who held onto stocks—even through volatile periods—did better in the long run. Investors ate up his advice, and his book, often called the "Buy-Hold Bible" helped convince a generation of investors to stay in the market through thick and thin. As you can imagine, I have a few things to say about this.

Check Out the Publication Date

When did Siegel publish his first edition of *Stocks for the Long Run*? In 1994, during that beautifully long market rise we talked about in Chapter 7. To be fair, Siegel has published updated editions since then, but it was his 1994 book that became the blueprint for many buy-holders. And why not? As we've discussed, buy-hold worked during that unusually long period of prosperity.

> But this long run is a misleading guide to current affairs. In the long run we are all dead. Economists set themselves too easy, too useless a task if in tempestuous seasons they can only tell us that when the storm is long past the ocean is flat again.
> —John Maynard Keynes, economist

It's History, Not the Future

Siegel did his analysis based on historical data, and acknowledged that no one can predict the future. "Economics is not an exact science, and human behavior can never be forecast with precision," he said in the preface to his book. "Scientists can predict the paths of celestial objects flawlessly for the next thousand years, but no one has consistently been able to foretell what will happen to the market just one day, not to say one hour, in the future. But it is just this unpredictability which makes the market so fascinating and challenging."

Unpredictability may be fascinating and challenging for a clinician, but as a financial advisor I am fascinated and challenged by the opportunity to minimize or mitigate that unpredictability so I can help my clients achieve peace of mind. Having a sell strategy can do just that, because investors know they have a certain point where they will get out of the market.

> *No one has consistently been able to foretell what will happen to the market just one day, not to say one hour, in the future.*
>
> —*Jeremy Siegel*

Siegel Also Admitted...

As we all know, market unpredictability can make investing risky. In terms of risk, Siegel found that other investment strategies carry less risk than buy-hold. He noted that an investor following the 200-day moving average strategy (which we discuss in Chapter 19) would have avoided the Great Crash of 1929 and the crash of 1987. So why does he prefer buy-hold over the moving-average approach? Because he believes that investors who use the moving average strategy to avoid those crashes would miss out on some of the gains that resulted from the market bouncing back.

To me, missing out on a few gains seems better than riding a bear market all the way to the bottom. The difference in the amount of money an investor could make is so marginal that I think most of us would give it up in order to avoid losing massive amounts. And remember, the goal of a sell strategy is to get the highest rate of return with the least amount of risk possible. Siegel's data shows that we would get 79 percent of the gains (net of transaction costs) while only being in the market 63.6 percent of the time. To quote Jeremy Siegel: "This means that on annual risk-adjusted basis, the return on the 200-day moving average strategy is still impressive, even when transaction costs are included." I'll take that any day.

Siegel may be the king of buy-hold, but it sounds like he agrees with me in a number of ways: The future is unknown, the market is unpredictable, and if you want to protect your principal, buy-hold may not be your best strategy.

The Market's (and Investors') Irrational Exuberance

Like me, Robert Shiller, 2013 winner of the Nobel Memorial Prize in Economic Science, doesn't seem to be a fan of buy-hold. In his now-classic book, *Irrational Exuberance* (a term Alan Greenspan used to describe the market in 1996), Shiller predicted the collapse of the tech stock bubble. Like Siegel, Shiller's timing was great: His book came out in 2000, right before the Dow peaked, then spectacularly crashed. Though Shiller did write in order to sound the alarm bell about the tech-market bubble, he said that in the end his book was really about "the behavior of all speculative markets, about human vulnerability to error, and about the instabilities of the capitalist system."

Because of these behaviors and instabilities, Shiller thinks that investors need to be more aware of risks. "We have already seen that stock price declines have not been that transitory," he wrote, "that they can persist for decades, and thus that long-term investors should see risk in stock market investments." In other words, stock prices can go down for a long time, and investors need to be aware of the risk they take if they decide to buy-hold.

> The market can stay irrational longer than you can stay solvent.
>
> —John Maynard Keynes, economist

Shiller believes that market risk and the subsequent need to protect assets are too often discounted, especially by the media. In a section where he suggests that the public should be helped to hedge risks, Shiller writes, "The personal investment media typically feature the opinions of celebrity sources who are apparently already rich and who subtly suggest that their advice might make one rich, too. It would be inconsistent with this fantasy to start talking about the mundane task of defending the value of the assets one already has. Those in the media and the investments community do not want to risk disturbing the get-rich fantasy, which they have learned to exploit to their own advantage." I think Shiller is correct in his assertion that the media has no vested interest in spending time talking about protecting against losses. The conversation doesn't feed into the get-rich fantasy they're selling.

Maybe it was this get-rich fantasy which kept most people from listening to Shiller about the tech bubble until it was too late: "Most of what I remember is people cheerfully and with apparent interest listening to my talk and then blithely telling me that they did not particularly believe me," he writes in the preface to the 2005 edition of *Irrational Exuberance*. "Some kind of collective conclusion had been reached about the stock market—and it had a powerful hold on people's minds." Later, after the stock market boom abruptly ended, this hold turned destructive. "I remember having breakfast with a woman and her husband at the very end of 2000, when the market was down substantially from its peak, the tech stocks down more than 50 percent. She said she did the investing for the family, and in the 1990s she had been a genius. He agreed. Now she confided, her self-esteem had collapsed. Her perception of the market was all an illusion, a dream she said. Her husband did not disagree."

But though people suffered during the recent bear markets, Shiller believes they are still overconfident. From the preface to his second edition (2005): "I do not know the future and I can't accurately predict the ups and downs of the markets. But I do know that, despite a significant slip in confidence since 2000,

> *I do not know the future and I can't accurately predict the ups and downs of the markets.*
>
> *—Robert Shiller*

people still place too much confidence in the market and have too strong a belief that paying attention to the gyrations in their investments will someday make them rich, and so they do not make conservative preparations for possible bad outcomes."

People think the stock market was created to make them money. It wasn't. It was created to help businesses raise money. If businesses don't grow, or if the economy stalls during a recession, the value of investments declines. Everyone who invests in the market should understand that the market goes down as well as up, and that protecting against the inevitable drop is just prudent.

The Emperor's New Clothes

I want you to know what the top economists think so as to give you some perspective. I think these are smart guys with fascinating ideas. I think their ideas make for interesting conversation that the media loves. And I think their theories are not relevant to the average investor. As they readily admit, all of their studies still don't allow them to foretell what the market is going to do tomorrow.

Valuations Schmaluations

I think many experts are misguided, too. I recently debated a fellow guest on the Fox Business TV show *Cavuto*. He argued that everything is sunny, there are no problems, and the current market has nothing but upside. When I said I believed we're building up a huge government infusion bubble with all the debt run up around the world, he countered with, "But valuations are not that high right now, so we shouldn't worry."

Investopedia.com defines *valuation* as "the process of determining the current worth of an asset or company." Most of the time, when people talk about valuations, they are looking at the PE ratios, the future earnings potential of stocks. If the PE ratio is high, stocks are expensive. If the PE ratio is low, stocks are cheap, which is what investors want.

I also heard Laszlo Birinyi, a market analyst I highly respect, say that we're not in a bubble because valuations are cheap, historically speaking. But how does he know they're inexpensive? As compared to what?

In October of 2002, after the tech bubble had burst, the market had gone down 49 percent from the highs in March of 2000. The market lost half of its value and, at the bottom, on October 9, a number of analysts and experts said the valuation of the market was 25.

The market then rose by 89 percent over the next five years, until December 31, 2007.

What did these same analysts estimate the valuations to be that month? 15! The valuations were lower before the big crash in December of 2007 than they were at the bottom of the market in 2002 after it had fallen 50 percent. How can it possibly be? This is ridiculous to me. The market goes up 89 percent and valuations are lower than they were before the rise?

And remember what was happening during the time of those 2007 valuations? Banks and mortgage companies were making loans and writing mortgages. They made tons of money, and their valuations were not particularly high because everyone anticipated their profits would continue to grow. But those profits were based on an illusion. Once that was exposed, the profits disappeared and the valuations became ridiculously high. A lot of the banks and mortgage companies went out of business. Others saw their stock drop by 90 percent.

Who Should You Listen To?

I don't listen to economists. I don't listen to analysts. After millions of dollars spent on computer systems and thousands of hours of study, even these very smart people cannot foretell the future. No one knows which direction the market will go. If you had listened to those experts who defended valuations in 2007, you'd have stayed in the market and lost money.

> If you want to know what's happening in the market, ask the market.
>
> —Japanese proverb

Who do I listen to? The market. It tells us when it's going up or going down. When we told our clients to get out of the market in November 2007, we weren't paying attention to economic theories. We didn't base our move on valuations. Our decision was driven purely by the direction of the market. The trend had turned in the wrong direction, so we sold.

I don't think you have to keep up on the latest economic theory in order to protect your investments. The market has a way of confounding even the most savvy of prognosticators and computer systems, which is why I don't believe you should use them to guide you.

I think you need to look at the direction of the economy and the direction of the market. I think you need to stop listening to bad buy-hold advice. I think if you want to retire without worrying about running out of money, you need a buy, hold, and SELL strategy.

Chapter 9

The Multimillion-Dollar Argument for a Buy-Hold-SELL Strategy

As a teenager, I spent a lot of my free time in financial planning seminars. Really.

My mother was an accomplished investor who was always looking for learning opportunities. When she found an interesting seminar, she dragged me along. I have to admit I didn't particularly enjoy the presentations, but through osmosis I picked up some good information. I also learned about the preeminent investment philosophy, the strategy that every smart investor should follow, which was of course, buy-hold.

Later, when I decided to make financial planning my career, I heard the same advice over and over. All the financial planning classes I took taught us to hold on to stocks. All the literature I read said that investors should follow the buy-hold path when building a retirement portfolio.

My teachers, the media, the experts—they all chanted the same buy-hold mantra:

- Be a long-term investor.
- Diversify.
- Buy high-quality companies.
- Rebalance periodically.
- Do all that, and your job is done.

Don't get me wrong; some of that is good advice. You should have a diversified portfolio, purchase stock in high-quality companies, and rebalance your portfolio. But is that enough? Can you just make good decisions, hold on to your stocks and wait for everything to turn out fine? Even though I had been initiated into the buy-hold brotherhood at an early age, I had some misgivings from the very beginning.

My Personal Experience with Buy-Hold

In December of 1972, there was a terrible stock market crash. The market fell 46 percent in 21 months, finally bottoming in September 1974. America's economy was in a terrible recession (many of you may remember the oil embargo, stagflation, and the misery index). My mother had followed the prevailing buy-hold advice, but she saw big losses during the crash and I saw the way those losses affected her, the anxiety she suffered. Although I was still in high school, I was old enough to know that something was terribly wrong.

Then when I was 30, we had the biggest stock single-day market crash in the history of the stock market. On October 19th, 1987, the market plummeted 20 percent in one day. To put this into perspective, if the Dow Jones Industrial Average were at 16,000 points today, a 20 percent drop would be about 3,200 points—all in one day! There I was, 30 years old with my life savings invested in stock mutual funds, and the stock market had its biggest single day drop ever. If that was not bad enough, the market continued to drop. As you can imagine, it made quite an impact on me. I had saved 10 percent of everything I had ever earned (by my mom's directive) and I saw years of savings vanish in just a few trading days. That event, combined with the memory of my mother's angst over her losses in the 1970s, gave me a healthy skepticism for the buy-hold strategy. I started actively searching for an antidote to buy-hold. I subscribed to all kinds of newsletters. I attended financial planning seminars. Bit by bit, I found strategies that didn't include holding onto stocks forever. I studied the advice of industry leaders who shared my distrust of buy-hold, and using their ideas as springboards, began to put together my own buy-hold-SELL strategy.

The Birth of a Sell Strategy

After that initial bear market in 1987, the market did fairly well during my early career. Although I was skeptical of buy-hold, I knew it worked fine when the market was going up, so I had no sense of urgency about completing my buy-hold-SELL strategy. Then, in the late summer and early fall of 1998, Russia experienced a debt crisis that threatened to have a global impact. The market dropped precipitously, and that drop rekindled my desire to create a sell strategy. I went back to work on my buy-hold-SELL idea. By 1999, it was good to go. In October of 2000 my strategy met the sell trigger, but because I had never used it in practice, I was reluctant to try it with all of our clients. However, as the market continued to fall, we moved more of our clients out of the market. By 2001, many of my clients were watching the market drop from the sidelines.

We weren't the first to tout a buy-hold-SELL strategy. Many of the existing strategies, though, had been created for traders who liked to watch the market every second and who didn't mind jumping in and out of the market all the time. My firm's clients are retirees who just want to avoid massive losses. So, in a way, our strategy was a "first." And even though I had back-tested the strategy and had every confidence in it, I was a little nervous when we implemented it. I felt like the first guy to test the parachute—I'm sure he was confident it was going to work, but I bet he held his breath when he jumped out of the airplane.

Avoiding the Market Crash of 2008

We advised our clients to get back in the market in April of 2003, when we hit our "buy" trigger, and they stayed there until November of 2007. That's when our strategy told us to advise our clients to sell again. It's also when I told the listeners of my radio show, *Money Matters with Ken Moraif*, and the subscribers to my *Market Alert* email newsletter to get out of the market. And you all know what happened next—the big crash of 2008. At that time, my firm managed about $700 million. If all our clients had stayed in the market (which at one point was down 57 percent), the losses that they would have incurred could have amounted to many millions of dollars. I believe I also helped out many listeners of my radio show and subscribers of my newsletter. I feel proud that my advice may have helped many people protect their retirement investments.

And I think those folks who were out of that bad market saved more than just money. I believe there are two components to the problem of buy-hold. The first and most obvious is the risk of enormous loss. The people who promote buy-hold admit that investors will probably experience huge losses, but say that diversification will mitigate the losses, and over time the market will come back and investors can rebuild their portfolios. But even if those buy-hold myths were true, that advice ignores the second problem with buy-hold: the psychological pain that accompanies loss.

In late 2008, I spoke with a gentleman who was considering becoming a client. He had recently lost enormous amounts of money in the market, and was very angry and depressed. In fact, he was so upset that he took it out on me and spoke to me in rough language and was really aggressive. I actually made a note in my file that I never wanted to see him again, and didn't want him as a client.

Two years later, I saw this gentleman's name on my calendar. "I thought I told you I didn't want to see this guy," I said to my assistant.

"But he was insistent," she said, "He apologized profusely for the way he acted during your last meeting, and said he wasn't like that normally."

And he wasn't. When I saw him again he was a completely different person. He explained that he had lost so much money in the 2008 bear market that he'd become depressed. "It ruined my life," he said. "I just froze. I couldn't listen to the radio or watch TV. I had almost a year's worth of statements stacked up—I was too afraid to open them. I holed up in my house, didn't leave except to go buy groceries. I was incredibly angry about my losses, and I took it out on my coworkers and my wife.

I became abusive, and she finally left me. After I met you I even lost my job."

He went on: "I got therapy. I got a new job and I'm starting my life over. I want to be a client because I don't want to have to go through that again. That loss destroyed me completely. I lost everything: I lost my job, I lost my wife, I lost my investments. I almost lost my sanity. It was horrible."

That poor guy went through an enormous amount of pain—and he was still working. He had an income. Imagine what might have happened if he'd been retired and had no wages to fall back on. It might've been too much for him to endure.

When you're an investor who's holding through a bear market, you don't just watch your stocks drop. You also have to endure the anguish of seeing your retirement goals go down the drain. I don't want you to go through that psychological pain. I don't want you to have to watch your retirement slip away. I want you to understand that buy-hold is not your friend, that the advice you've heard for years is nothing but a bunch of myths that can disrupt your retirement and even ruin your life. I want you to break free of the buy-hold myths.

Part Two

THE BUY–HOLD MYTHS: THE ADVICE THAT COULD RUIN YOUR RETIREMENT

Chapter 10

Buy-Hold Myth #1:
The Market Always
Comes Back

"**H**ang on to your investments," say the buy-holders. "Don't worry if your stocks drop. You're a long-term investor, and the market always comes back."

The market always comes back? Who says it will? When will it? Let's ask the Japanese.

Back in the late 1980s, the Japanese were wealthy. They were buying all our golf courses. Everyone held up Japan as the preeminent economy. They said, "Wow, look how great Japan is doing. We should copy them."

The Nikkei, Japan's stock market, peaked at 38,916 on December 29, 1989 (see Figure 10.1). It's never come back. It's still down about 64 percent from its apex in 1989. The Japanese stock market hasn't fully recovered, and it's been 25 years!

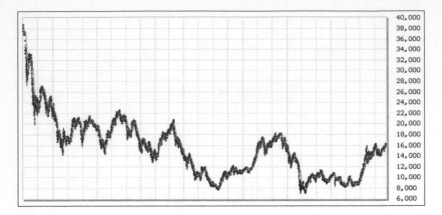

Figure 10.1 Japan's Stock Market Peaked in 1989 and Is Still Down 25 Years Later

"Wait a minute, Ken," you may say, "That's the Japanese. We're not Japan. We are the United States of America. That won't happen to us. We always find a way. American ingenuity can overcome all."

Let me tell you a little story:

Orphan Annie was asleep in her bed when a noise woke her up. A shadowy figure stood over her dresser—doing what? Breaking into her piggy bank! Annie turned on her bedside lamp.

"Leapin' lizards!" she said. "Daddy Warbucks! You scared me half to death! What are you doing with my piggy bank?"

"I'm sorry, Annie," said Daddy Warbucks, "but we just had a terrible stock market crash. All my money is tied up in the market. I just need a little bit of money to tide us over until the market comes back. I'll repay you then."

"Sure thing," said Annie, "When do you think that will be?"

"Soon," said Daddy. "Surely 1930 will be a better year."

Five years later, Annie woke up again. This time she recognized the figure breaking into her piggy back.

"Daddy Warbucks! What are you doing? You haven't repaid me from the last time you borrowed money."

"I know, Annie. But we just need to wait a little longer. You know what they say during times like these . . . "

"The sun will come out tomorrow?"

"The market will always come back."

"Okay," said Annie, and went back to sleep.

Many years passed, and yet once again, Annie, was awoken by the sound of someone shaking coins out of her piggy bank. She flipped on the light.

"It's been over 20 years, Daddy! I thought you'd repay me ages ago."

"Me, too, Annie."

"I thought you said the market always comes back!"

"That's what everyone told me," said Daddy Warbucks sadly, putting Annie's last nickel in his pocket.

Orphan Annie and Daddy Warbucks may be fictional characters, but the situation was real. In August of 1929, the Dow was at 380. Over the next three years, it went down to 54. That's an *86 percent drop!* People who stayed in the market, people like our friend Daddy Warbucks, long-term investors who bought and held believing that "the market always comes back"—those folks saw 86 percent of their money vanish. No kidding.

"No need to worry," the experts told them, "Keep the faith. The market will come back." And sure enough, the market did come back. It did, dear reader. But do you know how long it took for the market to rise above 380 again? Twenty-five years (see Table 10.1). The market didn't

Table 10.1   Bear Markets since 1929 and the Years to Break Even

Bear Market Dates	Duration in Months	% Decline	Years to Break Even
9/1929–6/1932	33	−86	25
9/1932–2/1933	6	−41	1
7/1933–3/1935	20	−34	2
3/1937–3/1938	13	−60	9
11/1938–4/1942	42	−46	6
5/1946–6/1949	37	−30	4
8/1956–10/1957	15	−22	2
12/1961–6/1962	6	−28	2
2/1966–10/1966	8	−22	1
11/1968–5/1970	18	−36	3
1/1973–1/1974	21	−48	8
11/1980–8/1982	20	−27	2
8/1987–12/1987	3	−34	2
7/1990–10/1990	3	−20	1
3/2000–10/2002	31	−49	7
10/2007–3/2009	17	−57	6
Average	18	−40	5
Excluding 1929	17	−37	4

SOURCE: S&P 500 Index prices obtained from Bloomberg.

come back until 1954, 25 years later. So, sure, the market may come back. But how many of you want to wait 25 years? And remember, if you are taking money out of your investments to live on, you may have depleted your savings. That money will never come back.

> That men do not learn very much from the lessons of history is the most important of all the lessons of history.
>
> —Aldous Huxley, writer

Some Big Bad Bears

"But you are talking about the Great Depression," you may say. "That happened just once in the history of our country." You're right. That enormous drop happened once, and the wait for that particular rebound was the longest in our history. But we've had several devastating markets that took enormous lengths of time to bounce back. Let's look at some of the biggest baddest bear markets:

- **1973.** The 1973 bear market lasted two years. The market dropped 48 percent. Investors lost almost half their money, and it took eight years to get back to even from that bear market.
- **1937.** The market dropped 60 percent in 1937. The actual bear market lasted just a year, but it wasn't until 1946 before investors got back to even—nine years in all.
- **2000.** I bet you'll remember this one: Y2K. This particular market also dropped 49 percent, but the bear lasted two and half years. Do you know how long it took for the market to come back to where it had been in 2000 before the drop? Seven years. It finally came back in 2007.
- **2007–2009.** You'll recognize this bear, too: It began in 2007, continued through 2008 and went into 2009, lasting about one and a half years. That market drop was a 57 percenter, and it wasn't until 2013 that the market got back to its previous high—almost six years later. Interestingly, the market reached a value it hadn't seen since

the year 2000. You could make the argument that it took 13 years to get back to even from the bear market of Y2K.

- **1929.** As you recall, the granddaddy of all bear markets dropped 86 percent. This particularly bad market lasted about three years and investors had to wait 25 years to get back to even.

The Smaller Bears Are Dangerous, Too

I've listed the five worst bears. I may not have included the ones that were "only" drops of 25 or 30 percent, but they can be just as devastating to your financial planning. After all, do you want to lose 25 percent of your money? And if you did lose it, would you live long enough to come back to even? Remember, if you are living on your investments, you would not be at break-even. The previous discussion assumes that you did not take any money out.

You may have noticed that two of the worst bear markets happened in recent memory. Does it appear to you that things are more volatile these days and risks are greater?

And let me ask you another question: Can you afford to risk even one of those bear markets? I may have listed some of the worst markets during the past hundred years, but consider this: Some floods happen only once in a hundred years, too. But if you're not ready for that hundred-year flood, it will wash you away.

Mini-Myth: If You Just Study Past Market History...

"But surely history is instructive!" you may say. "We can learn from our past mistakes." Of course we can and we should. But unfortunately, people parlay this truth into a buy-hold mini-myth. "If we just study the past," they say, "we can see that the market always comes back. It's much more consistent than people realize." True, to a point. But it pays to be careful when looking backward.

> Trying to predict the future is like trying to drive down a country road at night with no lights while looking out the back window.
> —Peter Drucker, writer/professor/management consultant

Some financial experts apply their current strategies to past data. They say, "We've got this new strategy, and we can show you that if it had been used in the past, you would have had tremendous gains." This method, called "backtesting" can yield interesting results. For example, several years ago, David Leinweber, the director of The Center for Innovative Financial Technology at Lawrence Berkeley National Lab, found a great predictor of the S&P 500's performance: butter production in Bangladesh. That's right, according to Leinweber's research, during the 10 years between 1983 and 1993, "when butter production was up 1 percent, the S&P 500 was up 2 percent the next year. Conversely, if butter production was down 10 percent, you could predict the S&P 500 would be down 20 percent." Wow. Knowing that, you should dispense with all financial analysis and intelligent thought and use the butter production in Bangladesh index to predict what the market will do. I'm kidding, of course. That's ridiculous. Leinweber was not giving us a great new market indicator, he was pointing out that backtesting can be manipulated to "prove" nearly anything.

It's very easy to go back and find ways to create portfolios that might have worked in the past. In fact, let's do just that. Let's time travel back 10 years. I have the perfect strategy for you, one that would have made you 32 percent per year for the past 10 years. It's a simple portfolio, with only two investments: Treasury bills and Apple stock. In our scenario, all you have to do is watch Apple. Every time the stock hits a new all-time high, sell it. Put that money into treasuries so you can make some interest. Then once Apple stock drops 10 percent, buy it again. Now let's come back to the present day. Wasn't that a fantastic portfolio? If you had followed that strategy over the past 10 years, you would have made 32 percent per year. That's great, but so what? Does this mean Apple and treasuries will make you 32 percent over the next decade? Maybe, but then again, maybe not. The past doesn't dictate the future.

> Prediction is very difficult, especially if it's about the future.
> —Niels Bohr, physicist

Mini-Myth: Time Is Your Friend

What was true in the past is not necessarily true in the present, either. "Time is your friend," say the buy-holders. That was true when you were 18. But if you're retired or going to retire next year, time is no longer your friend—in fact, it's your enemy.

Remember, the buy-hold experts who write about time and investments aren't thinking about you, the retired investor. They're thinking about the market, in the long term . . . and I do mean *long* term. I recently read an article entitled "Portfolio Risk Appears to Diminish over Time." In this article, the authors looked at years 1926 through 2010. That's 74 years. How many of you have 74 years to work with?

Why do the buy-hold people go back more than 70 years? Why don't they just talk about the past 10 or the past five years? Because if they did, it wouldn't satisfy their argument. The past decade has not been good. The Yale International Center for Finance reported that from 2000 through 2009, the average annual return for all stocks was a dismal −0.51 percent. Even the Great Depression was better: During the 1930s, the average annual return was −0.22 percent.

Homeland Security

Buy-holders may also argue that the past decade was anomalous, and that the market nearly always has positive returns over a 10-year period. That's fine if you're speaking in the abstract, but in the real world, if it happened once, it can happen again. And if you get caught in such an event, you can't decide to ignore it just because it's an anomaly. If you make a mistake, the penalty is severe. You can't afford to be wrong even once.

> Disasters can happen at any time. In fact, what makes them disasters is we're not expecting them. If we were expecting them, they wouldn't turn into disasters.
>
> —Zvi Bodie, Professor of Management
> at Boston University

We have only had one September 11 tragedy, thank heavens. The odds of another airplane being flown into a building are really, really small, but Homeland Security still makes us take our shoes off and go through the detectors and take our laptops out of our bags. Why? Because they can't afford to allow even one more event to happen. They can't say, "There's only been one event like September 11 in our country's history, so let's ignore the whole thing. It's not going to happen again." As a retired investor, you can't think that way, either. You need to be your own homeland security. You have to protect your investments as if they are your homeland. The fact that the market went up a hundred times in a row doesn't matter: What you need to worry about is the one time that is going to cost you.

INVESTMENTS AND
FINANCIAL SERVICES

Copyright 2003 by Randy Glasbergen. www.glasbergen.com

GLASBERGEN

**"The bull has finally returned, but your barn has
fallen apart and there's no grass in the meadow."**

SOURCE: Randy Glasbergen.

Mini-Myth: The Most Successful Investors Stay in for the Long Run

Can you wait for the market to come back? Can you be a long-term investor? Simply put, I say "no." When experts talk about "long-term investing," most of them mean investment cycles of 30, 50, and even 70 years. They also assume that investors won't spend any of that money—that they'll leave it in their accounts, ride out the storm, and wait for the market to come back. Imagine a retired person saying, "Okay, I'll wait out the 2008 market. I'll wait six years before I touch any of my investments, because taking my money out now violates buy-hold, which everyone knows is the smart way to invest. So I'll leave my money in the market. I'm not going to touch it. I'm also not going to eat, drive my car, or pay my mortgage for four years. I'm going to wait for the market to turn around." This is ridiculous, right? Only people with alternative sources of income can wait for the market to come around. If you're retired, that's not you.

Retired investors need to think about their time horizons. When I sit down with potential clients, the first thing I want to know is when they will need to access their money. The answer tells me that client's time horizon. Most retired people draw money out of their investments soon after they retire. They're not long-termers. If they make the mistake of thinking they are long-term investors, they often take more risk than they should. Let's say a retired investor decides she has a 20-year time horizon. The next month, bam! The market drops 30 percent. Uh oh. Any rational person knows that if you lose 30 percent of your money, you can't continue to spend at the same level. Our investor now needs to make a choice: slash her expenses by 30 percent, or recognize that the amount of time her money should last will be shortened dramatically. Not a pretty picture either way. It's very difficult to cut expenses by 30 percent. She'll either have to make huge changes in her lifestyle, or she will run out of money.

We're Not 25 Years Old Anymore

I do not climb ladders. I do not climb on the roof of my house. I do not climb trees. Why not? I have known too many middle-aged (or older) people who think they are still 25 years old. They climb up on their roofs to fix the gutters, and wind up falling and breaking something. I've learned from others' experiences (and a few of my own) that I'm no longer made of rubber and don't spring back the way I did when I was 25. I could break, and I might break in a way that would be permanent. It would be irresponsible for me to take that risk.

Risk is different when you're young. When you were 25, you probably didn't have a lot of money, so a 30 percent loss wouldn't change your life (and you would have had time to recoup that loss). Now, you've done a good job of saving your money and have built up enough to keep you comfortable in retirement. If you suffer a 30 percent loss today, you have broken something, and may have done irreparable damage.

I am not the same person I was at 25, and neither are you. We don't party the same way we did at 25. We don't dance the same way, play the same way, or travel the same way (YMCA, anyone?). We do very few things the same way at 55 that we did at 25. Why should investing be any different?

Where's the Contract?

Even if you are a 25-year-old investor reading this book (and if so, I congratulate you on your forward thinking), you should still be wary of the idea that markets always rebound to new highs. Where's the contract that says the market must come back? I've never seen it. I *have* seen the disclaimer on every investment sheet that shows any kind of return: "Past performance is not a guarantee of future results." There's a reason why that statement is required to be on those documents: It's true. You cannot use the past to predict the future. The market does not have to come back.

Just ask the Japanese.

Chapter 11

Buy–Hold Myth #2:
Don't Miss the 20 Best
Trading Days

Uncle Jed was smoking his corncob pipe on the porch of his mansion when his nephew rushed up waving a couple of brochures. "Yee haw!" said Jethro. "We are gonna invest in the stock market, and we are gonna clean up!"

"Well, doggies!" said Jed. "That sounds like a fine plan. How's it work?"

"Mr. Drysdale explained it all to me," said Jethro. "All we do is buy some investments, stick to our guns, and ride out the market. He called it 'buy–hold.'"

"That's all we do?"

"Yep. We just hafta make sure we don't miss the 20 best days and we'll be sittin' pretty. Lookee here," he thrust a brochure at his uncle. "It's all right here."

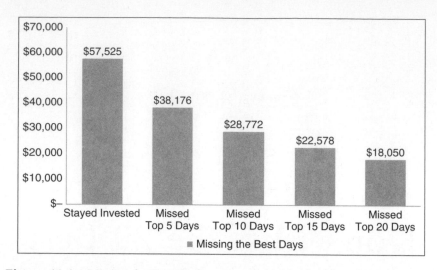

Figure 11.1   Missing the Best Trading Days (initial investment of $10,000)
Source: S&P 500, 1985–2010.

Jed pulled on his pipe and studied the chart in the first brochure (as shown in Figure 11.1).

"Just look at that!" said Jethro, looking over Jed's shoulder. "Only a durn fool would miss those 20 good days. You gotta stay in the market so you can catch 'em."

"Hmmm," said Jed, puffing away on his pipe.

"Look at this other one, too," said Jethro, handing another brochure to his uncle (see Table 11.1).

"So what do you think, Uncle Jed?"

"Appears to me that they're sayin' if we put our money in the market, we got to hold it there for the best trading days, or we miss out on making a bunch of money."

Table 11.1   Don't Miss the 20 Best Days

Period of Investment	Average Annual Return of S&P 500 Index
Stayed invested	9.14%
Missed top 5 days	6.93%
Missed top 10 days	5.43%
Missed top 15 days	4.14%
Missed top 20 days	3.00%

Source: S&P 500 Index, 1985–2010.

"That's right!"

"I reckon that's a good idea. But did Mr. Drysdale tell you when those best days happened?"

Jethro shook his head.

"Or when the worst days happened?" asked Jed, looking through the papers on his lap. "I think Mr. Drysdale's left out some pretty important information."

"Oh shoot," said Jethro.

"Yep," said Jed, handing the brochures back to his nephew. "Seems like buyin' into this buy-hold idea is sorta like buyin' a pig in a poke."

A Pig in a Poke

Buying "a pig in a poke"—buying something unseen on the sellers' say-so—isn't the smartest course of action. You'd better check to make sure there's a really nice pig in that poke (bag), if that's what you're paying for. And if you're considering a buy-hold strategy, you should check out the accompanying advice, too.

The "don't miss the 20 best market days" myth comes in a variety of shapes and sizes. But, as Jed asked, when did those days happen? And when did the worst trading days happen? Shouldn't you have all the information before believing this buy-hold myth?

When Were the Best Days?

To begin our exploration of this myth, let's take a look at Table 11.2 and the best trading days in a 25-year period.

What do you see when you look at these dates? Are you beginning to see a trend? Let's put the days in order by date, so the pattern becomes even more apparent (see Table 11.3).

Table 11.2   Best Trading Days (1985–2010)

1	10/13/2008	11.59%
2	10/28/2008	10.80%
3	10/21/1987	9.11%
4	3/23/2009	7.09%
5	11/13/2008	6.93%

(continued)

Table 11.2   (Continued)

6	11/24/2008	6.49%
7	3/10/2009	6.38%
8	11/21/2008	6.34%
9	7/24/2002	5.74%
10	9/30/2008	5.43%
11	7/29/2002	5.42%
12	10/20/1987	5.35%
13	12/16/2008	5.15%
14	10/28/1997	5.12%
15	9/8/1998	5.10%
16	1/3/2001	5.01%
17	10/29/1987	4.94%
18	10/20/2008	4.78%
19	3/16/2000	4.77%
20	10/15/2002	4.74%

SOURCE: S&P 500 Index.

Table 11.3   Best Trading Days by Date (1985–2010)

12	10/20/1987	5.35%
3	10/21/1987	9.11%
17	10/29/1987	4.94%
14	10/28/1997	5.12%
15	9/8/1998	5.10%
19	3/16/2000	4.77%
16	1/3/2001	5.01%
9	7/24/2002	5.74%
11	7/29/2002	5.42%
20	10/15/2002	4.74%
10	9/30/2008	5.43%
1	10/13/2008	11.59%
18	10/20/2008	4.78%
2	10/28/2008	10.80%
5	11/13/2008	6.93%
8	11/21/2008	6.34%
6	11/24/2008	6.49%
13	12/16/2008	5.15%
7	3/10/2009	6.38%
4	3/23/2009	7.09%

SOURCE: S&P 500 Index.

Yep. With the exception of one day, October 28, 1997, all of the "best" trading days were caused by bear markets. To catch these best days, you would have needed to be in the market during the terrible1987 collapse, during the tech-bubble crash, and during the great bear market of 2008–2009. Interesting.

Riding the Market during the Best Days

"But," some of you may be thinking, "if I can catch those best trading days, maybe it's still not such a bad idea to ride out a bear market."

Okay, let's say you were invested between Sept. 29, 2008 and March 23, 2009. You would have caught 10 excellent trading days. They weren't just 10 of the 20 best days in the years on our chart (1985–2010) but were 10 of the 20 best trading days of all time. If you were in the market during that time, you would have hit half of the best trading days ever. You would have also experienced a 36 percent drop in the market. Congratulations! By being in the market for just six months, you hit 10 of the best trading days in the history of the stock market. Your reward? Losing 36 percent of your money.

The Worst Trading Days (So Far)

We've only explored half of this myth so far. As Jed asked in our story, what about the worst days? When did they occur? See Table 11.4.

Table 11.4 Worst Trading Days (1985–2010)

1	10/19/1987	−20.45%
2	10/15/2008	−9.02%
3	12/1/2008	−8.92%
4	9/29/2008	−8.78%
5	10/26/1987	−8.26%
6	10/9/2008	−7.61%
7	10/27/1997	−6.86%
8	8/31/1998	−6.80%
9	1/8/1988	−6.75%
10	11/20/2008	−6.70%
11	10/13/1989	−6.11%
12	11/19/2008	−6.10%

(continued)

Table 11.4   (Continued)

13	10/22/2008	−6.09%
14	4/14/2000	−5.82%
15	10/7/2008	−5.73%
16	1/20/2009	−5.27%
17	11/5/2008	−5.26%
18	11/12/2008	−5.18%
19	10/16/1987	−5.15%
20	11/6/2008	−5.01%

SOURCE: S&P 500 Index.

Some of the market's worst days have made history. October 19, 1987 was christened "Black Monday" after the market plummeted more than 20 percent. It was the worst trading day in history, and if you were in the market during that time I bet you remember it. But do you remember October 16, 1987? Or October 26? Those days also rank as some of the worst trading days in history (see Table 11.5). The 2008–2009 bear

Table 11.5   Worst Days by Date

19	10/16/1987	−5.15%
1	10/19/1987	−20.45%
5	10/26/1987	−8.26%
9	1/8/1988	−6.75%
11	10/13/1989	−6.11%
7	10/27/1997	−6.86%
8	8/31/1998	−6.80%
14	4/14/2000	−5.82%
4	9/29/2008	−8.78%
15	10/7/2008	−5.73%
6	10/9/2008	−7.61%
2	10/15/2008	−9.02%
13	10/22/2008	−6.09%
17	11/5/2008	−5.26%
20	11/6/2008	−5.01%
18	11/12/2008	−5.18%
12	11/19/2008	−6.10%
10	11/20/2008	−6.70%
3	12/1/2008	−8.92%
16	1/20/2009	−5.27%

SOURCE: S&P 500 Index.

market included a slew of bad days, too: 12 of the 20 worst trading days in our 25-year period. Do you see another pattern emerging?

It's not just the best trading days that occur as a result of bear markets. Out of the 20 worst days, only three of them, January 8, 1988, October 13, 1989, and October 27, 1997, were not caused by bear markets. Seventeen out of 20 were the result of bear markets. That's 85 percent. If we have a really bad trading day, the odds are that we're in a bear market. And if you're in that market, the odds are that you lost an enormous amount of money.

Avoiding the Big Bad Bear Days

If you could miss the worst days, you could protect your investments from some hefty losses. And believe it or not, avoiding those days might actually add value to your portfolio. Let's take another look at that last chart in our story, the one that highlighted the losses incurred if investors missed the best days (Table 11.6). Let's compare it against another chart in Table 11.7 which shows the impact of missing some of the worst days.

Looks like it might be more important to miss the worst days, doesn't it? A 2007 study by professor of financial management Javier Estrada

Table 11.6 Missed the Best 20 Days

Period of Investment	Returns
Stayed invested	9.14%
Missed top 5 days	6.93%
Missed top 10 days	5.43%
Missed top 15 days	4.14%
Missed top 20 days	3.00%

SOURCE: S&P 500 Index, 1985–2010.

Table 11.7 Missed the Worst Days

Period of Investment	Returns
10 days	12.87%
20 days	14.64%
40 days	17.53%

SOURCE: S&P 500 Index, 1985–2010, Hepburn Capital Management 2010 Study.

also considered the effect of missing both the best and worst days across 15 equity markets and over more than 160,000 trading days. Estrada found that missing the best 10 days resulted in portfolios 50.8 percent less valuable than if the investors had just bought and held their stocks. He also found that missing the worst 10 days resulted in portfolios that were 150.4 percent more valuable.

Wow, 150.4 percent. That's great! We should all make sure to be in during the best trading days and out for the worst ones.

If only we could.

Doing the Impossible

If you could somehow catch the best days while avoiding the worst ones, you'd be a hero. There'd be monuments built for you on Wall Street. But it's not humanly possible. As you've learned by reading this chapter, the majority of both the market's best and worst days were in bear markets. Not only that, they cluster around each other. Take a look at Table 11.8.

The 2008 bear market is a prime example of this mixture of worst and best. During October 2008, Lehman was collapsing. The market dropped 7.61 percent on October 9, and then rebounded, giving us that

Table 11.8   Best/Worst Trading Days (1985–2010)

10/16/1987	−5.15%
10/19/1987	−20.45%
10/20/1987	5.35%
10/21/1987	9.11%
10/26/1987	−8.26%
10/29/1987	4.94%
1/8/1988	−6.75%
10/13/1989	−6.11%
10/27/1997	−6.86%
10/28/1997	5.12%
8/31/1998	−6.80%
9/8/1998	5.10%
3/16/2000	4.77%
4/14/2000	−5.82%
1/3/2001	5.01%

(*continued*)

Table 11.8   (Continued)

7/24/2002	5.74%
7/29/2002	5.42%
10/15/2002	4.74%
9/29/2008	−8.78%
9/30/2008	5.43%
10/7/2008	−5.73%
10/9/2008	−7.61%
10/13/2008	11.59%
10/15/2008	−9.02%
10/20/2008	4.78%
10/22/2008	−6.09%
10/28/2008	10.80%
11/5/2008	−5.26%
11/6/2008	−5.01%
11/12/2008	−5.18%
11/13/2008	6.93%
11/19/2008	−6.10%
11/20/2008	−6.70%
11/21/2008	6.34%
11/24/2008	6.49%
12/1/2008	−8.92%
12/16/2008	5.15%
1/20/2009	−5.27%
3/10/2009	6.38%
3/23/2009	7.09%

SOURCE: S&P 500 Index.

fantastic trading day on October 13. Then it dropped again on October 15 and presented us with another nice rebound on the 20. The market continued to bounce up and down all the way until March 2009.

And look once more at October 1987. October 16 was one of the worst 20 days. It was followed by the biggest market drop to date on October 19. But we had a nice gain (5.35 percent) on October 20, and a 9.11 percent gain on the 21st. Then the market fell precipitously on October 26 (−8.26 percent), and rose back up 4.94 percent on October 29. The whole month of October 1987 was like a best day/worst day sandwich. If you had been trying to catch the best days in the market during that time, you would have actually lost money.

"The stock market fell sharply today, then bounced back, spiraled upward, jumped forward, leaped to new heights, tumbled rapidly, and took first place in a gymnastics competition."

SOURCE: Randy Glasbergen.

You can see that the best and worst trading days happened randomly and are very difficult to predict. Just for fun, let's say you are good enough to be able to pick those random days. You actually can figure out what twenty days will be the best trading days and which 20 days will be the worst. To catch the best days and avoid the worst, you'd have to jump in and out of the market, over and over. Take October 2008 as an example. You'd want to be in the market for that great trading day on October 13 (11.6 percent), then jump out to avoid the bad day on October 15 (–9 percent). But better get back in the market so you catch October 20 (4.8 percent), out to avoid October 22 (–6.1 percent), and back in again to get that 10.8 percent rise on October 28. You couldn't do it. It can't be done.

And there's no way you could predict which days were going to be good or bad. The best and worst days did cluster closely together, but they were not necessarily in succession.

No, the only way to have hit the best trading days was to be in the market during those bears. Ninety-five percent of the best trading days (and 85 percent of the worst days) were in bear markets.

We've been talking about recent market history, but let's look at the top 20 best trading days of all time shown in Table 11.9.

Table 11.9 Top 20 Best Trading Days of All Time

Rank	Date	% Change
1	10/30/1929	12.53
2	10/06/1931	12.36
3	09/21/1932	11.81
4	10/13/2008	11.58
5	10/28/2008	10.79
6	09/05/1939	9.63
7	04/20/1933	9.52
8	10/21/1987	9.10
9	11/14/1929	8.95
10	08/03/1932	8.86
11	10/08/1931	8.59
12	02/13/1932	8.37
13	12/18/1931	8.29
14	02/11/1932	8.27
15	07/24/1933	8.14
16	06/10/1932	7.66
17	06/03/1931	7.54
18	05/15/1948	7.54
19	11/10/1932	7.51
20	10/20/1937	7.48

SOURCE: S&P 500 Index.

All but one of those days (May 15, 1948) were a result of bear markets. Sixteen of them were caused by the Great Depression. If I polled a million people, I bet not one, not even the most uninformed person in the country, would want to be in the market during the stock market crash of 1929. You don't have to be an intellectual writing studies to know that sometimes you don't want to be invested in the market.

He's in the Wrong Lane!

Studies have their place, but you need to use them sensibly. For example, there may be hundreds of studies that demonstrate that wearing seatbelts saves lives. Knowing that, you wear a seatbelt. But if you're traveling 70 miles an hour down the freeway and see an 18-wheeler barreling toward you in the wrong lane, do you stay the course because you're wearing a seatbelt? Do you say to yourself, "Studies have shown that I'll survive a crash if I wear my seatbelt, so I'm not going to get out of the way of that 18-wheeler?" Of course not. You may be wearing a seatbelt, but you still need to take precautionary measures, especially when it comes to out-of-control 18-wheelers. The same thing goes for your investments and out-of-control bear markets. Keeping your money safe can save you from a lot of suffering.

I believe that people who tell investors to stay in a bad market so as not to miss the best 20 days discount the emotional suffering that accompanies financial loss. Investors experience pain when they lose money. Some of them can't sleep at night if they lose 2 percent. Imagine how a 90 percent drop, like the crash of 1929, could affect them. I don't want my clients to ever experience that.

Missing the Best and Worst

Luckily, there is a way to possibly avoid the angst that accompanies a bear market. By predetermining a trigger point based on historical data, you can create a sell strategy that puts the odds in your favor, giving you a good chance of missing both the best and worst days (more about this strategy—and why it's *not* about predicting the market—in Chapter 18).

> *The way to win the game of investing is by not losing.*
>
> *—Ken Moraif*

The way to win the game of investing is by not losing. I advised my clients to get out of the market in November 2007. Those who followed my direction missed eight of the top ten best trading days. And you know what? I don't care. You know why? Because they also missed five of the top 10 worst trading days.

You may be thinking, "Okay, I understand that it's important to not lose money, but what about returns? If I got out of the market and missed both the best and the worst days, what would happen to my portfolio?"

If you had a 100 percent stock portfolio invested in the S&P 500 Index and missed the 20 best and the 20 worst trading days from 1985 to 2010, your return would be 10.63 percent per year (see Table 11.10)!

And remember, returns are "gravy" when you're retired. Your main job is to protect your principal, not to chase returns and risk losing 55

Table 11.10 S&P 500: 25 Years Ending December
31, 2010, Average Annual Return 7.39%

Miss Both Best and Worst	Returns
10 days	10.56%
20 days	10.63%
40 days	10.56%

SOURCE: Hepburn Capital Management 2010 Study.

percent of your investments in a bear market. Retirement should be a time when you enjoy the fruits of years of hard labor. You should be relaxed. You should enjoy yourself. You should play tennis, go to the beach, and spend time on your hobbies. If you stay in the market hoping to hit those 20 best days, you'll be in the market during turbulent times. You won't be relaxed. You'll be stressed. You won't sleep.

And even worse, you would be going through all that trauma for nothing. You can't hit the 20 best days. The Mr. Drysdales of the financial world have created an interesting academic exercise that can't be duplicated in real life. Sure, if you could travel back in time, predict what the stock market would do, and act accordingly, you'd get great returns. And if you could travel at the speed of light, you could get to the moon in 1.25 seconds. True, but so what? It's an irrelevant argument. No one can be "out" for only those 20 best days and "in" for the rest. It's an argument designed to keep you invested during bear markets.

Hindsight is always 20-20.

—Billy Wilder, filmmaker

Chapter 12

Buy-Hold Myth #3:
Don't Be the Fool Who
Sells at the Bottom

In 2011, the average equity fund investor underperformed the S&P 500 by 7.85 percent. Dalbar, the nation's leading financial services marketing research firm, found that the typical equity mutual fund investor suffered a loss of 5.73 percent, while the S&P 500 gained 2.12 percent. In a March 2012 press release, the Dalbar researchers said, "They (investors) decided to take their losses instead of risking further declines. Unfortunately, as is so often the case, this occurred just before the markets started on a steady trek to recovery."

Sounds like those investors were fools who sold at the bottom of the market, doesn't it? According to Dalbar, which conducts similar studies each year, this is not unusual behavior. Investors get nervous when the market drops. They may tell themselves to stay the course because they're long-term investors, but they feel the loss of every cent as the market plummets. Eventually, they can't take the anxiety anymore. They panic and sell, often near the bottom of the market. And since history tells us that the market bounces back nicely the first year after a bear market, those investors lose out on the typical rebound. By reacting emotionally, the "fools who sell at the bottom" are shooting themselves in the foot. These investors, indeed, would have done better in the market had they stuck with buy-hold.

Am I saying that "don't be the fool who sells at the bottom" is bad advice? No. I'm saying that you don't want to be the fool who sells in a *panic*. Big difference.

This particular myth is dangerous because there is some truth to it. Selling at the bottom is obviously a bad idea. But buy-holders use this advice to keep investors from selling at all. They also keep investors in the market with two similar mini-myths: "You don't want to miss the rebound," and "The rebound is equal to the fall." They say straight out that anyone who gets out during a bear market is foolish. I think it's their arguments that are foolish.

Mini-Myth: You Don't Want to Miss the Rebound

Those who say "Don't be the fool who sells at the bottom..." often conclude their argument by saying, "After all, you don't want to miss the rebound."

If you follow a sell strategy that gets you out of bad markets, you could miss a rebound. It's true. But if you're retired, remember that protecting your principal is your number-one job. A defensive strategy, even when it doesn't give you the returns you might have made, protects that principal. One bear market could destroy you, robbing you of an average of 37 percent of your life savings. An enormous loss like that could change your life, especially if you're retired.

"What's the matter, girl? Is Timmy's portfolio in trouble?"

SOURCE: Randy Glasbergen.

By sticking with the buy–hold philosophy in order to catch a rebound, you may put your retirement at risk. You have to choose: Would you rather miss a market rebound, or would you rather take shelter and protect your life savings? See Figure 12.1.

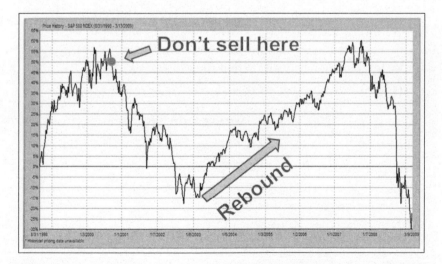

Figure 12.1   Don't sell here, because you'll miss the rebound.

Mini–Myth: The Rebound Is Equal to the Fall

"But," you may say, "Some of these rebounds are fantastic, In fact, I've heard that the rebound is typically equal to the fall. Where's the risk?"

It's true, after the market sinks to its lowest point, the rebound can be very, very big. After the market bottomed in March 2009, it went up almost 90 percent over the next year. But there are risks. To catch that rebound in 2009–2010, you would have had to endure 2008. You would have seen half your money vanish, not knowing if the market would turn around, and you would have needed to stay in the market until the very bottom to capture that wonderful rebound. Emotionally, that's not easy to do. Most people just can't take it. They panic and sell. By sticking with a bear market, you risk falling prey to your emotions.

> "If you sacrifice security for growth, you risk losing both."
> —Ken Moraif

And even if you have incredible intestinal fortitude, how low do you go? How far do you ride the market down, hoping for a rebound? In 2008, the market dropped 57 percent. Those who panicked and got out of the market at that point sold at the bottom. But during the Great Depression, the market went down 90 percent. Investors who got out back then, when they were down "only" 57 percent, probably thanked their lucky stars they had sold when they did.

Quick Quiz: Where's the Bottom?

Question: How can you tell when the market hits bottom?

A. The market is very undervalued.
B. All the investors capitulate, and there are no more sellers.
C. There is no more optimism left.
D. You have lost all of your money.

Answer: D. Though the other answers could be true, they're based on perception and are impossible to diagnose correctly. Only D is definite. When you've run out of money, the market has bottomed, as far as you're concerned.

There is another substantial risk in riding the market down in order to catch the rebound. Market drops and rebounds are measured in percentage terms. Even if you lost half your money and the market rebounded 50 percent, you wouldn't be back to even. Many people don't understand this concept, including one of the fools in our next story.

The Two Fools of Mayberry R.F.D.

Barney sang, "Oh, I'm gon-na make mon-ey, and it's gon-na be big..." He suddenly stopped and scratched his head. "Hey, Andy, what's a good rhyme for 'big'?"

Andy leaned back in his chair. "Well, there's 'pig'..."

"Pig?"

"Or 'wig,'" said Andy, "But tell me. How are you going to make big money?"

"Well, I've got 100 dollars invested in the market..."

"How about that? I do, too," said Andy.

"And the market's dropping..."

"That doesn't sound good."

"No, it's great!" said Barney, "Because I'm going to ride it down and catch the rebound! And it's gonna be big!"

"You know, Barn, I'm going to get my money out of the market."

"Now, Andy, that's just plain foolish. You'll miss the rebound."

"I'll take my chances," said Andy.

A few months later, Barney was singing again. "If I hold on-to my stocks, in time they'll grow big..."

"Never finished that song?" said Andy.

"Still working on it."

"Still in the market, too? I'm glad I got out. It's down 50 percent."

"I know," said Barney. "I only have 50 dollars right now. But I don't want to be the fool who misses the rebound, like some I might know." He looked sideways at Andy, who didn't seem to notice. "Besides, I'm not worried. The market is gonna come back and its going to be..."

"Big," said Andy. "Right."

A year later, Barney burst into the sheriff's office. "I told you, Andy! I told you so!" he said. "The market came back and I made 50 percent!"

He cleared his throat. "There's gotta be something that rhymes with 'percent.' "

"Fifty percent," said Andy. "Sounds good on the face of it."

"What do you mean, 'on the face of it?' I made 50 percent! How much did you make?"

"One percent," said Andy.

"You should have listened to me. I told you getting out of the market was foolish."

"Uh, Barn, how much money do you have now?"

"Let's see, I lost 50 percent, so I had just 50 dollars . . ."

"Right . . ."

"Then I made 50 percent, so I made . . ." Barney started to count on his fingers.

"Fifty percent of 50 dollars . . ."Andy prompted.

"Oh! Twenty-five dollars."

"So now, you have . . ."

"Fifty plus 25 . . . I have 75 dollars! Oh." Barney's face fell. "I have 75 dollars. How much did you say you made?"

"One percent."

"And you have how much money now?"

"One hundred and one dollars."

Barney shook his head. "Guess I'm the fool, even after making 50 percent. Beats all, Andy, beats all."

Which Fool Would You Rather Be?

After reading that story, would you rather be the investor who stayed in a bear market, caught the rebound, and made 50 percent, or the one who made just 1 percent, but protected his principal? Which fool would you rather be?

I wouldn't call Andy a fool in that story. He may have sold, but he didn't sell in a panic. He decided that it was time to protect his investments, and did so without emotion. Most of us, though, don't have the strict discipline it takes to make a dispassionate decision when the market is falling down around our ears. We need to have a sell strategy, to know in advance when we'll sell, and what our trigger point will be.

Generals plan ahead so that they don't make rash decisions in the heat of battle. Investors shouldn't make emotional decisions in the thick of a bear market, either.

When you have a strategy, you can make a plan without being driven by your emotions. When we advised our clients to sell in November of 2007, nobody was panicked yet. Things looked bad, but nobody was freaking out. Nobody thought it was the end of the world, but because we had decided in advance what our trigger points were, we got out of the market.

We weren't fools who sold at the bottom. We were practical investors who got out before it got bad because we had a sell strategy. Buy-holders assume investors have no strategy. They assume that investors who sell do so because they can't take the trauma of losing enormous amounts of money. And yes, those who sell in a panic are fools. But those who protect their investments during bad times are just the opposite.

Chapter 13

Buy-Hold Myth #4: Diversify Your Portfolio . . . That's All You Need to Do

One evening after coming home from work, Rob fell over the ottoman, righted himself, and looked up to see his wife Laura crying. "Don't worry, honey, I didn't hurt myself. You know I always trip over that darn thing, and I'm always okay."

"That's not why I'm crying."

"Do you want to tell me why?"

Laura sniffled. "You'll be mad at me."

"No, I won't."

"Oh, Rob, I've been a snoopy-nose."

Rob waited.

"I opened your mail," said Laura. "The letter from our financial advisor."

"Oh, honey," Rob said, giving her a kiss. "That's *our* mail, not mine. It's okay."

"No, it's not! We're down a lot of money!" Laura said, bursting into tears again.

"Listen, don't worry. Our portfolio is diversified, so we should be fine. It's probably just a mistake. I'll call Mr. Smith tomorrow and set up an appointment. Okay?"

The next day, Rob and Laura sat in front of their financial advisor.

"Don't worry," said Mr. Smith, "You're well diversified, and it's worked wonders for you."

"I'm so relieved," said Laura. "So we haven't lost any money?"

"The market dropped 50 percent, but your portfolio went down only 30 percent."

"Thirty percent?!" Rob jumped up out of his chair. "Did you say we lost 30 percent?"

"I don't see why you're so upset," said Mr. Smith, "I thought you'd be thanking me. As I said, you could have lost 50 percent, but . . . "

"But we *only* lost 30 percent?!!" said Rob. "We're paying you a fee to help us lose money and we should thank you?"

"Oh, Rob!" said Laura.

Many investors put their faith in diversification, believing that it will buffer their investments against bear markets. Unfortunately, as Rob and Laura found out, they're only partially right.

Put Your Eggs in Different Baskets

Don't get me wrong. Diversification is a good investment strategy. By filling your portfolio with various types of investments that behave differently in the same market environment, you can reduce your risk. In a perfect world, when one of your investments goes down a dollar, a different one goes up a little more than a dollar. This "negative correlation" is the basis of diversification. For example, bonds tend to go up when stocks go down, and vice versa, which is why it's good to have a blend of these assets in your portfolio.

We use mutual funds and ETFs to help our clients diversify their portfolios, advising a blend of U.S. large-cap growth stocks, large-cap value stocks, small-cap growth stocks, and small-cap value stocks, all of which tend to perform differently, even during the same time period. We also diversify by geography by including stocks from Europe, Asia, Latin America, and other places around the world, as they act different from the U.S. market. We include bonds in the mix, which are also diversified with U.S. treasury bonds, U.S. corporate bonds, and foreign bonds. We then balance the foreign bond section of our portfolios by choosing bonds from across Europe, Japan, and the emerging market countries. We make sure all of our eggs aren't in one basket.

By spreading your risk across various asset classes and styles of investing, you can smooth the bumpy ride of the market. Even a bull market can be an emotional roller coaster, dipping up and down as much as 19 percent. Investors who are diversified feel the downs less dramatically, since diversification tends to mitigate that downside. Take a look at the chart in Figure 13.1. You can see that a diversified portfolio (the gray line) didn't lose as much in the great bear market as the undiversified portfolio (the black line). You can also see that both portfolios went down.

Figure 13.1   Balanced Index Portfolio

Diversified Index Portfolio (60/40) is a mix of 35 percent Russell 3000 Index, 17 percent MSCI EAFE, 3 percent MSCI EM, 40 percent BarCap Agg, and 5 percent FTSE NAREIT Index. Indexes are unmanaged and cannot be invested in directly.

SOURCE: S&P 500.

A nondiversified portfolio is like a racecar. It can be a fast ride, but boy, you really have to work that stick shift. You have to shout over the engine noise. You feel every little bump in the road. Once we retire, most of us prefer a more relaxed ride. Diversification gives us that extra bit of comfort.

**"I have a diversified retirement plan:
30% hopes, 30% wishes, 40% prayers."**

SOURCE: Randy Glasbergen.

A Junk Drawer of Investments

But most investors diversify haphazardly. They see an analyst on television who tells them they should buy ABC stock, so they do. They read an article in a financial magazine touting "the Top 10 Mutual Funds of the Decade," so they buy the top four in the magazine's list. They listen to their bankers who advise them that the cash sitting in their accounts would be better invested in XYZ company, so they buy that stock. Little by little over the years, they accumulate a bunch of different assets. That amalgamation of assets doesn't necessarily provide investors with the risk reduction they would get from a properly diversified portfolio, but it does provide a false sense of security. They feel like they're diversified, but instead they've created a junk drawer of investments.

Even worse, investors listen to people who tell them to close the junk drawer. "Because you're properly diversified," the buy-holders say, "you can sit back in your hammock and sip mint juleps, and your portfolio will take care of itself." Sounds great to the investors, who then follow that advice, shut their drawers, and dream of opening them years later to find them overflowing with cash. But think about the investors who followed that advice in 2007. When they came back in 2009, their junk drawers weren't overflowing. They didn't even have the amount of money they had in 2007. In fact, some of those investors' drawers were nearly half empty.

Copyright 2003 by Randy Glasbergen.
www.glasbergen.com

**"I strongly advise you to diversify your portfolio.
That way it will take longer to figure out
how much you've lost."**

SOURCE: Randy Glasbergen.

Believe it or not, some financial advisors really do believe it's okay to lose money in a bad market. In 2008, I read several articles that offered advice about helping clients cope with the bear market. The number one tip? Remind clients that they are diversified. Sure, diversification did mitigate investors' losses during the bear market. But it wasn't enough. Unfortunately, it's impossible to find investments that are negatively cor-related all of the time. Between 2007 and 2009, almost every asset class went down. Even a well-diversified portfolio didn't save investors who stayed in the market.

Diversification Isn't Enough

Steve and Danno were buy-holders who "invested for the long-term." Steve had $250,000 invested in a properly diversified portfolio. Danno also had $250,000, but he had invested in an index that exactly mirrored the S&P 500. Then the 2008 bear market hit.

The chart in Figure 13.2 shows that diversification worked. Steve, the properly diversified investor, ended up with $31,520 more than Danno. But both investors still lost money. They started with $250,000, and in just one bear market, Steve was out nearly $100,000, and Danno lost over half of his investments.

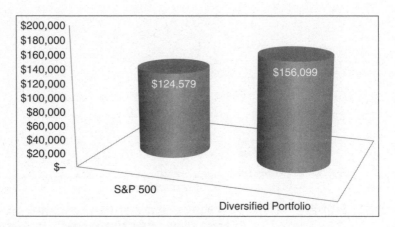

Figure 13.2   Diversified Portfolio after the Fall
Note: Value on March 2009 based on $250,000 initial investment on October 2007.
See appendix for diversified portfolio allocation.
SOURCE: GSAM; Ibbotson.

But being good buy-holders (and not having read Chapter 12), they believed their faith would be validated when they caught the inevitable rebound after the bear market was over. As the chart in Figure 13.3 shows, the rebound was fantastic. After 18 months Steve made 48 percent and Danno made 39 percent. You'll note, though, that even after 18 months neither investor had recouped their original investment.

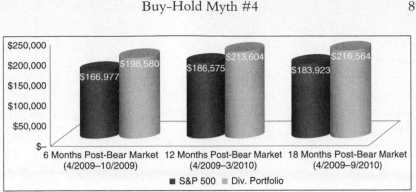

Figure 13.3 Diversified Portfolio—The Rebound
See appendix for Benchmarks and Blend allocation.
SOURCE: GSAM; Ibbotson.

This example didn't account for Steve and Danno taking living expenses out of their investments. Nor did it account for inflation or taxes. If they had been typical retirees who needed their investments to live on during those years, they would have been in trouble.

Buying a Drill Bit

When you go to the hardware store to buy a drill bit (the piece of metal that fits on the front end of your drill), what are you really buying? You're buying a hole. You don't really want that piece of metal. That piece of metal is a pain in the neck. You have to store it somewhere, you have to find it when you need it, it has to be the right size . . . You don't want all that fuss, you want the hole. The drill bit is just a tool, a means to an end.

Diversification is a tool, too. You really don't want a bunch of different stocks and bonds and treasuries. You don't even want green paper with zeros all over it. You want security, freedom, convenience—all the things that money buys. And though diversification can be an efficient tool, in bad times, it may not give you what you need. There were many periods during the past 80 years in which diversification was not enough.

We experience a bear market every three years on average. Every three years, you stand a chance to experience substantial losses, losses that may be mitigated by diversification, but are still significant. Do you want to take that chance with your retirement? When it comes to your financial security, diversification is an incomplete strategy. It's a "spread-your-risk plan," not a "get-out plan." You need both. In bad times, cash is king. The only way to avoid losing money in a bear market is to be out of the market.

Diversification does work. You should diversify by putting your eggs in more than one basket. But you should also be prepared to grab those baskets and run if a bear comes along.

Chapter 14

Buy-Hold Myth #5: You Won't Make Any Money If You Sell and Sit in Cash

L et's play a game. I'll put a plank of wood—300 feet long and three feet wide—in the parking lot. In the middle of the plank I will place a thousand dollar bill. I'll dare you to get on one end, walk to the middle of the plank, pick up that bill, and walk to the other end. If you get to the far end of the plank without falling off, you can keep the thousand dollars.

If I offered you this challenge, would you take it? Of course you would. Why wouldn't you? But what if I took that plank of wood to the Petronas Towers in Kuala Lumpur and anchored it between the two towers, 88 stories high? I'd even put a rock on the bill, to keep the wind from blowing it off. Would you still take my dare? No? Why not? Your investment in both situations is the same: a 300-foot walk. The return on your investment is the same: a thousand dollars. Your investment and return are the same in both circumstances, but one challenge you would take and the other you would not. What's the difference? The second dare has 88 stories of risk underneath it. You could die.

SOURCE: Fotolia.

What if I increased the prize to a hundred thousand dollars? Or a million? Would you walk that plank, 1,483 feet above the ground? (you're not allowed to wear a parachute, by the way). Most of you would still decline and you'd be right to do so.

Some people knock my idea of selling in a bad market. They point out the fact that my clients will make zero while they're out of the market and in cash. So what? If there were a danger my clients might lose half their money or more, I would advise them against that risk. I wouldn't tell them to walk across a 300-foot plank 88 stories up off the ground so they can make money. That would be irresponsible. I would try to keep them off the plank altogether. I would put them in cash.

Why Not Short the Market Instead of Getting Out?

When you short the market, you "borrow" stocks, betting that the market will go down. If it does, you could make money. But the reason we get out of the market is to minimize risk. Investopedia's definition of short selling notes that "the risk of loss on a short sale is theoretically infinite." Why would we take our clients out of the frying pan and into the fire?

Cash Can Be Your Friend

Poor old cash. Nobody likes cash. Nobody likes low returns. It is human nature to want to make the most money possible. We have pursued money for most of our adult lives. During our working lives we wanted raises. During our investing lives, we wanted higher returns. Cash doesn't offer that.

But if you are retired or retiring soon, you have to make friends with cash, and even with a 0 percent return. You can't be worried about making high returns. You have to protect your principal. One of the consequences of protecting your principal is that you will most likely underperform. It doesn't matter. Would you rather hold on while the market drops 6,000 points? Don't you think the retirees who experienced that sort of loss wish they had gone to cash? That they would have rather made zero than watch their net worth drop by 30 percent or 40 percent? Getting out of the market and into cash can save your retirement and give you peace of mind. Not only that, but making zero isn't such a bad deal.

Bewitched by Zero

"Oh, whatever is the matter now?" Endora cast a withering glance at Darrin, who sat at the kitchen table with his head in his hands.

"Mother," said Samantha, "Can't you be nice for even a minute?"

"Oh, all right. What's the matter, Derwood?" Endora poked Darrin with a fingernail.

"*Darrin* is worried about our investments," said Samantha. "The market seems to be going down."

"So?"

"We're both getting close to 65. We want to retire and be secure."

"Well, if that's what you want," Endora waved her arms above her head.

"Now wait a minute . . . " Darrin raised his head, too late.

Endora snapped her fingers. "Done."

"Oh, no. What did you do?" Darrin looked at his wife, who turned to her mother.

"I simply cast a spell on your investments," said Endora. "They'll stay at a nice even zero so you won't have to worry."

"Zero? Not worry? Are you kidding?" said Darrin. "Sam, please tell me she's kidding."

Samantha looked at her mother. "I don't think she's kidding."

"Of course not," said Endora. "Why would I do that?"

"Ohhh," Darrin groaned.

"Darling? Maybe it's not so bad," said Samantha, "Tell you what, I'll just take a little peek into the future and see what happens."

"No witchcraft . . . " Darrin stopped and put his head back down on the table. "Oh, go ahead."

Samantha wiggled her nose and shut her eyes. "Let's see . . . We won't need the money until you retire at 65 . . . then we'll need to take out money to live on."

Darrin groaned again.

"You'll want to take out 4 percent," added Endora. Darrin looked at her in disbelief. "I have been around the block, you know," she said.

"If we take out 4 percent of our investments for the rest of our lives . . . " said Samantha.

"Don't forget about inflation," Endora said. "You'll need to increase the withdrawal by an extra 3 and a half percent per year."

"Plus 3 and a half percent . . . " Samantha wiggled her nose again. "that money will last us . . . 19 years! We'll have money until we're 84."

"Really?" said Darrin, raising his head.

"Really, darling," Samantha said.

"Really," said Endora. "I don't know what all the fuss was about."

That's Not All

But our bewitched couple doesn't necessarily have to make zero forever. If there's an up year in the future, they could get back in the market and make more than zero.

Doing the right thing is always the right thing to do.

—Ken Moraif

Cash doesn't always make zero. In the early 1980s, the interest on cash was over 10 percent. The current low interest rate for cash is a historical anomaly.

It's likely that either the market will stabilize and/or cash will pay more than zero at some time. If it does, Samantha and Darrin will be able to extend the amount of time their money will last beyond age 84. There's only a remote chance that they will make zero for the rest of their lives, even if they were in cash the whole time.

And even if, like Samantha and Darrin, you do make zero for a short time, you know what? It's the right thing to do. Sometimes there's a cost, but doing the right thing is always the right thing to do. When you're retired, you need to be willing to take a lesser return in exchange for having money for the rest of your life.

Security or Surfing?

Let's say you have a beautiful vacation home right on the beach. As a lifelong surfer, this oceanfront house is a dream come true. One day, all the forecasters say there's a hurricane coming your way. You have two choices at this point: You can board up your house, get in your car and drive 100 miles north, or you can stay behind and say, "It'd be a total blast to surf those gnarly waves during the hurricane. That'd be cool." The first choice isn't glamorous and it's not fun. You've got to secure your house, drive for a few hours, and get a hotel—all for something you're not even sure will happen. The second choice is easier: You ignore the danger and get ready for some great waves. Let's say that in scenario number one, the hurricane doesn't hit the beach. It turns around and goes off to sea. You would have been better off staying in your house.

You could have spent time on the beach instead of being cooped up in some hotel. Darn it! Now let's say that you chose scenario number two instead and the hurricane does hit. You stayed behind and now you're dead.

Which is the better choice? Would you rather have the inconvenience and expense of playing it safe? Or would you rather stay and possibly get wiped out?

If you are retired, or about to retire, you cannot afford to take the chance of getting flattened by a financial storm. You can't walk a plank thousands of feet in the air. You can't risk your principal.

If you get out of the market and go into cash, you may not make as much as you could have, but you'll protect your principal. And remember, if you had to make zero for the rest of your life, you could take out 4 percent a year and live off your investments for 19 years. Making zero seems like a small price to pay for that kind of security.

> Money is better than poverty, if only for financial reasons.
> —Woody Allen, actor/filmmaker/comedian

Chapter 15

Buy-Hold Myth #6: You Haven't Lost Any Money Unless You...

No, I didn't forget to finish the chapter title. I started it, but I want you to finish it. You've probably heard this statement a hundred times: "You haven't lost any money unless you _____." If you're anything like my seminar attendees, you can finish the sentence without even thinking about it. When I ask this question, they shout out the answer right away: "You haven't lost any money unless you...*sell*."

This buy-hold advice is brilliant in its simplicity: "You haven't lost any money unless you sell." Do you want to lose money? Of course not. So you don't sell. You think you're safe that way. Until the day you look at your statement and see that you're down 50 percent, just like a certain garage mechanic...

Shame, Shame, Shame

Gomer's garage was going gangbusters. "Golly!" he said to his cousin Goober. "I think we're going to need another auto lift. I'm going to go downtown and take some money out of my account."

A little while later, Gomer sat in his financial advisor's office.

"You probably know that the market is down quite a bit right now..." said his advisor.

"It is?"

"About 50 percent."

"Golly!"

"But as you know, you haven't lost anything unless you sell."

"Phew. I sure am glad I didn't sell," said Gomer, "because I need some of that money right now."

His advisor cleared his throat and handed Gomer a statement. "As I said, the market is down..."

"Sure is lucky we didn't sell, isn't it?... Hey! What's this?" Gomer asked, pointing at the minuses on his statement. "This says I have less money than I did before."

"That's just a paper loss."

"Good," said Gomer, "let's go get my money."

"It's not that simple. You see, your money isn't in your account..."

"Where is it? Are you keepin' it in a drawer back there?"

"No."

"Do you mean I don't have that money anymore? You told me that if I didn't sell I wouldn't lose any money!" Gomer pointed a finger at his advisor. "I trusted you. Shame, shame, shame!"

I couldn't agree more. And I'm a little steamed. I have met so many people who lost so much money. I talked to one gentleman who lost $600,000 in 2008. He said he called his advisor nine times (nine!) and his advisor kept saying, "No, no, stay the course, don't do anything." This investor said his advisor told him, word-for-word, "Don't worry. You haven't lost any money unless you sell." "What do you mean?!" said the investor. "I haven't sold anything and I've lost $600,000!" He was outraged. He felt like he was being ridiculed. How could his advisor believe what he was saying when his client's portfolio was down more than half a million dollars?

"It's just a paper loss" really angers me. The whole idea insults my intelligence. What does that mean, "a paper loss"? What they want you to think is that you haven't lost any money. Not true. A paper loss is an actual loss. Like Gomer, if I want to take money out of my account, I can't take out the past or future value of my investments. That money is not in my account. It's only the current value I can draw on.

Mini-Myth: Future Appreciation

Some advisors hang their hats on "future appreciation." Once you sell a stock, they argue, you can't take advantage of its inevitable upswing. If you ever hear this argument, I'd suggest you look around for your advisor's crystal ball. How can he promise there will be future appreciation? What if there isn't? What if your stock keeps going down? There are no guarantees. Remember the employees of Enron? At the end they were actually locked out of their accounts. They couldn't sell even if they wanted to. Did they lose money? Yes, they did. They lost everything.

> The only thing we know about the future is that it will be different.
> —Peter Drucker, writer/professor/management consultant

The idea of *future appreciation* is tied to "the market will come back" myth. As we discussed in Chapter 11, no one can predict the future market. It may come back. It may not. It may come back, but take 25 years to do so, as it did after the Great Depression. And whether the market does or doesn't bounce back has nothing to do with whether you lost money. Those are apples and oranges. If someone combines those two ideas in one sentence—"You haven't lost any money because the market will come back"—they are saying they can predict the market. And in my opinion, if they tell you that you haven't lost any money unless you sell, they are lying to you. I contend that the

> *The way to* not *lose money in a bear market is to SELL.*
> —*Ken Moraif*

opposite is true: The way to *not* lose money in a bear market is to SELL. The only way to not lose money in a bear market is to not be in it. To do that, you have to sell.

A Flat-Out Lie

I know that "lying" is a strong word. In my view, though, if your account statement says you're down, you have lost money. Whether you have sold or not is irrelevant. If you look at your statement and there is a loss, you lost money. Period, end of sentence. Anyone who tells you differently is lying.

Some people tell you that you've only lost money if you sell so that you'll be afraid to get out of the market. Why would they want you to be afraid? Because if you sell, they stop making money.

Why They Don't Want You to Sell

Many investment houses benefit from investors staying in the market. If you are sitting in cash for a year, they are not making any money. Other advisors receive 12B-1 fees, which are ongoing fees based on investors' use of a mutual fund. If your advisor works on that fee structure, and you sell and go into the money market, your advisor gets no income. Effectively, by telling you to sell, your advisor has told you to stop paying him.

These firms and their advisors have a vested interest in convincing you to stay in the market. Imagine if they were paid for selling, rather than buy-holding. I think they'd sing a very different tune. I think they'd say, "You're losing money? Sell! Sell! Sell!"

I'm certainly not saying that all financial advisors are self-serving. Most want the best for their clients. I do think it is human nature, though, to convert a benefit to one's self into a benefit for others. No matter how honest they are, or how high their integrity, financial planners are swayed in the direction of the product or service or action that will make them the most money. They find ways to convince themselves that what is good for them is good for their customers.

They may truly believe that the market will come back, and that their clients' money will come back, too. That doesn't mean they're right. In fact, one study found that mutual-fund managers who held onto losing stocks fared worse than managers who cut their losses—by about four percentage points annually.

> Sometimes people hold a core belief that is very strong. When they are presented with evidence that works against that belief, the new evidence cannot be accepted.... And because it is so important to protect the core belief, they will rationalize, ignore and even deny anything that doesn't fit in with the core belief.
> —Frantz Fanon, psychiatrist

You want an advisor who is willing to cut losses when necessary, one who has no vested interest in whether you are invested in one product versus another, or in any investment versus cash. To make sure there is no conflict of interest, you need to understand how your financial planner gets paid. Ask your advisor (or prospective advisor) straight out, "Will you ever put me in cash?" If the answer is, "I will never put you in cash because I believe you should always be invested," you have your answer. If your advisor says, "Yes, I would get you out of the market if necessary," ask, "What happens to your income if I'm in cash?" If you learn that your advisor will not get paid if you are out of the market, you'll know that advisor will have a very hard time putting you in cash during bad times. It probably won't happen.

Why You Fear Selling

Behavioral-finance professor Terrance Odean of the University of California, Berkeley, has studied the behavior of investors who are reluctant to sell. Based on his research, he believes that the issue "isn't primarily about economic loss, it's about emotional loss." Investors, Odean thinks, want to believe that their original stock-buying decisions were good ones. Once they have to sell that stock below its purchase price, they can no longer tell themselves that they made a smart choice.

In my experience, people who feel they made bad choices suffer more than people who feel they missed out on opportunities. Let's use an example: Two people both have $100 to invest. One of them sits on the sidelines and misses out on a 25 percent rise in the market. The other person invests that $100 and, oops, the market goes down by 25 percent. Both of them lost $25—one by missing out on an opportunity, the other by losing money in the market. Which person do you think felt worse about their decision and its end result? I think most people feel the loss of actual money much more keenly than the loss of a potential gain, even when the dollar amount is the same.

It also appears that people feel the pain of losing more than the pleasure of winning. In an unpublished study led by Gregory Berns of Emory University, researchers studied the brains of people who were asked to hold or sell an investment. The researchers used a brain scanner to focus on an area of the brain known as the ventral striatum, which typically responds to rewards. They moved the prices of the participants' assets up and down, and watched their response. Interestingly, the subjects' reward centers did not show significant activity when a stock price rose. When the study participants were questioned later, many said they had hoped for a rise. The research suggests that the test subjects weren't surprised by their stocks gaining value and didn't feel rewarded, because the rises and rebounds in their asset prices were anticipated.

I've noticed this phenomenon. When stocks go up, people tend to think, "I knew that stock would go up. Boy, I'm smart!" There's not a big emotional reaction. They see the rise in their asset prices as a validation of their intelligence and good decision making. But when their investments go down, they feel it in a personal way. They feel like they made a bad choice, like they're not as smart as they thought they were.

When we're on top of the world, we think we're great. When things aren't working out for us, we think we stink. There is a quote from Rudyard Kipling above the gates at Wimbledon: "If you can meet with triumph and disaster and treat those two impostors just the same...." The wise person realizes that triumph and disaster *are* impostors and doesn't get swept away by either one, but it's tough to do. It goes against our nature.

Not only is it human nature to want to validate our choices, but our brains are geared to look for patterns. This behavior evolved to help keep us safe. "My friend was eaten by a saber-toothed tiger," thought the caveman. "That guy who lived in the cave over the hill was

> *Even though random can happen three times in a row, it's still random.*
> *— Ken Moraif*

also eaten by a saber-toothed tiger. The next time I see a saber-toothed tiger, I'm going to run." Though this sort of thinking may have saved us from being eaten by tigers, it can work against us. We sometimes latch onto patterns we think we see in the marketplace and think that the patterns repeat themselves exactly. Of course they don't, which is why nobody can predict the market. The market's ups and downs are often random. And even though random can happen three times in a row, it's still random. Ascribing certainty to a random event is not the wisest thing to do, but we were made that way for self-preservation purposes.

Our belief in patterns also helps convince us that our current situation will continue. Back in the late 1990s, during the great run-up of the tech bubble, the market was rising by 20 percent a year. I remember clients who would comb through their portfolios and say, "Anything not making at least 15 percent is a dog and I want to get rid of it." They had become accustomed to that particular market and thought it was going to go on forever. People feel the same way about bear markets: Whatever the current circumstance, that's the one people think will continue indefinitely.

When it comes to investing, you can see that our brains may work against us in several ways:

- We believe that our investments will go up.
- We feel like failures when our stocks go down.
- We look for patterns, and rely on them to tell us how to act.
- We believe that our current circumstances will continue indefinitely.

Add to that that the fact that we are wired to avoid pain, and you can see why we find it so difficult to sell, even when it's the right thing to do.

"My emotions and finances are Siamese twins attached at the Dow."

SOURCE: Randy Glasbergen.

Buying Stuff Is Fun

We do like to buy. As investors, we are conditioned to buy. We've been trained over years and years to work and save so we can invest, or, in other words, so we can *buy*. I believe this conditioning makes most investors brave when they buy and scared when they sell. And I believe that they'd be much better off if they could be the opposite.

I'm not saying you shouldn't buy, but that you should think carefully when you do. You should be a coward when it comes to buying. It is after you have bought an investment that you could lose money. That is where your risk lies.

But when you sell an investment, you get to keep what you have. You know the price you sold at and the amount that will end up in your account after you have sold. You have now eliminated all the risk in that investment because you do not own it anymore. I contend that the advisor who says, "You haven't lost any money unless you sell" has it backwards. As mentioned earlier, the way to protect yourself from loss when the market is going down is, in fact, to sell. Do it bravely.

Live to Fight Another Day

Being a brave seller isn't easy, especially if you've been a buy-holder. I know people who have never sold anything in their lives. How stressful would it be to suddenly change a strategy you've followed for 30 years? To get out of the market when all of your buddies are telling you to stick it out? To sell when your advisor tells you that you haven't lost anything unless you sell?

It can take courage to sell. You may not get back your original investment. But sometimes you have to cut your losses. A good general won't leave all his forces to fight an uphill battle. He won't sacrifice his troops when there's no hope of success. He will pull them back so that they will live to fight another day. He knows that winning the war is more important than victory in any one battle. As investors, we have to distinguish the battle from the war, and make sure we don't deplete our resources to the point where we don't have enough capital to continue the fight.

You can always get back in the fight later. Remember the nonsensical arguments about missing out on future appreciation and the market rebound? Those arguments imply that your stocks will come back and you'll miss out on great opportunities. But there is no law that says that if you sell, you can't buy back later. You're not prohibited from buying back your investments. If you sold a good asset because you couldn't afford any more loss, you can always buy it back, maybe even at a lower price.

By getting out of the battle and protecting your principal, you can make sure you have the means to buy back your investments. Yes, you may have missed out on potential gains, but you lived to fight another day. If you buy into the idea that "you won't lose any money unless you sell," you may feel okay about your investments until it's too late. You may avoid the pain of selling, but leave your principal at risk. You may feel fine, but you're living in denial. And living in denial can make you poor.

> *Living in denial can make you poor.*
> *— Ken Moraif*

The Real Answer

"You haven't lost any money unless you sell" is advice that is meant to keep you in denial and in the market. Not only is this particular advice a myth, it's a flat-out lie. The truthful way to state that sentence? "You haven't lost any money if your statement shows no loss." The mere act of selling is irrelevant.

Chapter 16

Bits and Pieces: More Buy-Hold Nonsense

I recently read an article where several buy-holders maintained that investors who got out of the market were fools. Let's take a look at their arguments:

Many investors sell because they're afraid, and end up getting out of the market at the bottom.

Sounds like that buy-holder believes that investors panic. Okay, I'll buy that.

They forget that history shows that the market always comes back.

Hmmm, that expert needs to read Chapter 10.

They need to stay in the market for the long term, for more than 10 years.

More than 10 years? This guy can't be talking to my clients. Retired people need to access their money now. Rarely can they wait 10 years to draw money from their investments.

For example, if they held for 20 years. . .

Whoa. Twenty years? This interviewee is not only dismissing over-50 investors, he's talking nonsense.

"Ten Years" Twaddle

As I've said earlier, investors over 50 years old can't afford to wait even 10 years, much less 20. They invested so that they could retire and have a nice life, not so they could sit and wait around for years before spending any of their money. You could argue that the buy-holders interviewed in the article were speaking to a younger audience, but I don't believe their advice holds water at any age. Do I want my 24-year-old daughter to buy-hold for 20 years? No way. I don't want her to lose half her money in a bad market, even if she *may* get it back in 20 years.

The idea of a 20-year holding period is fairly recent. Buy-holders used to tout 10-year periods. This past decade has taken the starch out of the 10-year time frame argument, so they've moved on to 20 years. What happens if we have a bad 20-year period? Will they advise us to hold onto our stocks for 30 years?

And, of course there's no guarantee that everything will be hunky-dory in 10 or 20 years. The world changes incredibly fast these days. What are the chances that the stocks you own now will still be good investments in the future? Look at BlackBerry. A few years ago, they made the business phone that everyone wanted. Now the iPhone may put them out of business. And Apple looks good today, but even that's not a sure bet, especially now that Steve Jobs isn't at the helm. Heck, Apple may not even be around in the future. Remember Montgomery Ward? Or how about that highly esteemed company named one of "America's Most-Admired Companies" by *Fortune* magazine six years in a row? What was that company's name? Oh yeah. Enron.

Can't We Just Use the P/E Ratio?

Many analysts use the P/E ratio as a reason to remain in the market. Let me explain why using market valuations can be a very dangerous way of deciding whether to stay in the market or to sell. The P/E ratio is the price of a stock divided by the projected earnings of that stock. The price of the stock (the P) is easy to find, so there's never any argument about that. That number is the numerator. The denominator, the E, is the projected earnings. That number is an analyst's estimate of a company's future earnings.

The larger the projected earnings, the bigger the denominator (E), which results in a smaller fraction, or ratio. The smaller the ratio, the cheaper (more underpriced) the stock price. And vice versa: the bigger the ratio, the more expensive (overpriced) the stock. To decide whether the stock market is expensive or cheap, the analysts create a weighted average, using every stock on the market.

If you asked a hundred analysts to give you today's P/E ratio and the forward earnings of the market, I bet you'd get a hundred different answers.

Copyright 2004 by Randy Glasbergen.
www.glasbergen.com

"Stocks fell sharply today on predictions of speculation of rumors of negative indicators."

SOURCE: Randy Glasbergen.

Why? Their answers are based (at least in part) on perception, since the E portion of the P/E ratio is an estimation of future earnings. Let's use Apple again as an example. If you asked those hundred analysts what Apple's earnings will be in the next year, I bet some would say, "Without Steve Jobs, Apple is no longer able to compete and will go in the tank for sure." Others would probably say, "No way! Apple stock will double in value." Still others would predict that Apple stock will remain the same. How do you decide who's right? You've got to pick one opinion, and if you're wrong—oops, there goes a big chunk of your retirement.

In fact, at the end of 2007 bank valuations were quite low because analysts expected them to continue making large profits on the subprime mortgages they were underwriting. Those bank stocks rapidly lost value in 2008, when the true value of those future earnings became known.

A Word about Warren Buffett

Many proponents of buy-hold use Warren Buffett as a good example of a buy-holder, praising him for sticking to his guns when his investments were getting slammed during the tech bubble. Warren Buffett is a great example of a businessman and investor, but he's not like you or me. Warren doesn't just buy and hold stocks; he buys *companies* and holds them. When Warren says you can ignore the market if you have stock in a good company, you have to realize that you can't know a company like he does. He is involved in the management of the company. I don't think many of us have that access and privilege.

Money Matters is my financial planning firm. I founded it and built it up with my own money. I'm an investor in this firm. As long as I work here and know what's going on, I'm confident in this company's future. I won't sell it during a rough patch because I believe in our team. I'm sure of our ability to play through bad times, to come out the other side and prosper. I have knowledge and control of my firm. Having that knowledge and control gives me the confidence to buy and hold my own company. It's not the same with my investments. I don't have the same control over the companies that I invest in. We can't compare Warren Buffett's investment philosophy to the typical investor's buy-hold strategy. They're apples and oranges.

And remember, there's a reason they call Warren Buffett "The Oracle of Omaha." He's one of the greatest investors of all time. He has a talent for choosing companies that have huge potential. The average person or mutual fund company doesn't have that skill. For that matter, no one in the world has Warren Buffett's talent. He's the Michael Jordan of the financial world. Saying that you can make money by emulating Warren

Buffett is like saying you can be a great basketball player by copying Michael Jordan. Just leap from the top of the key, fly through the air, and dunk the ball. All basketball fans would love to be able to play like Michael Jordan, but the reality is that no one can do what he does. Ditto with Warren.

By the way, Warren Buffett's investments lost 50 percent during the credit crisis. Yes, they did come back almost six years later, but why take such a large loss if you don't have to?

Part Three

BUY, HOLD, *SELL*: AN INTRODUCTION TO SELL STRATEGIES

Chapter 17

What's beyond the Buy-Hold Myth?

Now you realize that buy-hold advice doesn't make sense for retired investors. You understand the fallacies behind the myths. You know that:

- The market may take 25 years to come back—if it ever does.
- The market's 20 best days occur randomly. It's impossible to make sure you don't miss them.
- Selling doesn't make you a fool unless you sell in a panic.
- Diversification can buffer you against losses, but it can't save you.
- You may be better off sitting in cash than sinking in a bear market.
- You *can* lose, even if you haven't sold.

You know to avoid the buy-hold strategy, but what *do* you do? You create a plan that allows you to get out of the market at a predetermined point, without making an emotional decision. You create a sell strategy.

Not Market Timing

As a proponent of sell strategies, I've been called a market timer. I'm not. I'll be the first one to say you can't time the market. Besides the fact that there are too many variables and too much volatility, it's impossible to choose the perfect time to invest based on the market's behavior, so you should not even try. To illustrate my point, let me ask you a question: Would you rather invest when the market was going down, or when the market was going up? I bet you'd say, "I'd rather invest when the market was going up. I want to invest in a market that's rising." Now let me ask you the same question in a different way: Would you rather invest when the market was down, or when the market was up? Looking at it from that angle, would your answer be different? I suspect it would. In my experience, most people say they want to invest when the market is down, but invest when it is up.

Even If You Could...

Even if you could time the market, the danger to your investments would outweigh any benefit you might receive. Imagine there were two investors who had each decided to invest $2,000 per year for the past 35 years. Investor Number One invested in the S&P 500 Index once a year on the market's highest day each year. Investor Number Two bought at the market's lowest point each year. Which fictional investor do you think earned more money over the past 35 years? If you said Investor Number Two, you're right. The guy who invested at the lowest point each year would have ended up with more money. But guess what? That guy, Investor Number Two, would have had $519,000. Investor Number One, who invested at the market's highest point each year would end up with $498,000. That's a difference of just $21,000 over 35 years. That's nothing. There's no reason to try to pick the top or the bottom of the market each year to do that, especially when you may risk staying in a bad market to do so.

Trends and Tides

You can't sit on a beach and guess when each wave is going to crest. You can't predict the movement of every single wave. But you can tell whether the tide is receding or coming in. I believe you can do the same with the market. You can't time the "waves," but you can see the trends. When the 2008 market was dropping like a stone, did you think the tide was receding? Did you feel it in your gut? Absolutely you did. Your intuition can help you by alerting you to danger. But you should never make an investment decision based on intuition or emotion. You have to rely on quantifiable fact.

Chapter 18

The 200-Day Moving Average Strategy

O nce you know if the trend (the tide) of the market is upward or downward, you can use that information to your advantage. The 200-day moving average (200 DMA) uses mathematics to demonstrate the direction of the market. This trend-watching strategy shows you the actual overall trend of the market, removing the daily and/or weekly volatility so that you don't put too much emphasis on one bad trading day or even one down week.

Typically, if the market is above the 200 DMA, we are in a rising market environment. When the market dips below that average, we are in a declining one. By knowing the direction of the market, you can plan to protect yourself from large losses.

How to Calculate the 200-Day Moving Average

The 200-day moving average tells us the trend of the market by looking back over the previous 200 trading days (roughly nine months) and averaging the closing prices of those trading days. You can calculate the 200-day moving average by adding yesterday's closing price to the previous 199 trading days' closing prices. You'll come up with a large number:

Yesterday's closing price

+

Previous 199 trading days' closing prices
_____
Big number

You then divide that number by 200 to get the average for yesterday:

Big number/200 = Average for yesterday

Mark that point on a chart, and make another dot that signifies where the market closed yesterday.

Tomorrow, you will add today's closing price, and drop a day off the back end, so that you are again working with 200 days:

Today's closing price

+

Previous 199 trading days' closing prices
_____
Big number

Again, you divide by 200 to get the average for today. Then you plot both the average and the market on your chart. If you do that every day, you'll get a graph like the one in Figure 18.1 on the next page. The thick black line represents the S&P 500 and the gray line is the 200 DMA.

As you can see, this chart shows you the general direction of the market. The 200-day moving average measures the trend so that you can visualize it.

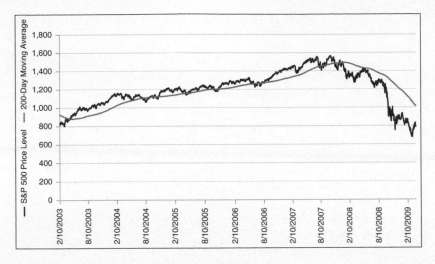

Figure 18.1   February 2003–February 2009

Criteria for Calculating the 200-Day Moving Average

- Make sure your calculations are based on objective mathematics, not subjective emotions.
- Use readily available data: You can Google "200-day moving average, today" and find easy-to-follow information on several sites. Any number of websites will even draw the graph for you—no math needed on your part.
- Apply your calculations to the entire market, not just a specific asset class. Don't complicate the formula with a lot of moving parts.

The 200-Day Moving Average in Action

By smoothing out the curve of the market, the 200-day moving average tells you whether the market is in a rising or falling trend. If the new days that you add on to your calculations are good days, the line that plots the 200-day moving average will curve up (see Figure 18.2).

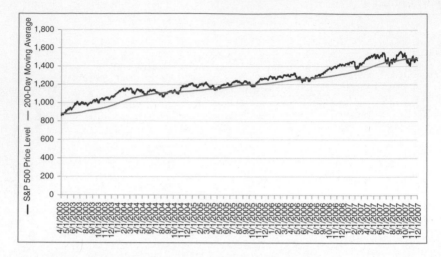

Figure 18.2   Bullish Period: April 2003–December 2007

If the closing prices you add on have declined from previous prices, the curve will begin to bend downward (see Figure 18.3).

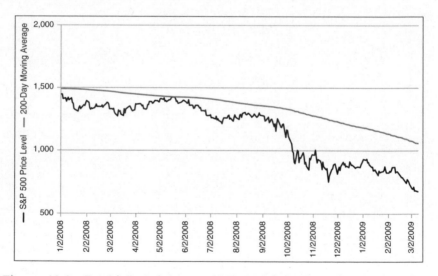

Figure 18.3   Bearish Period: January 2008–March 2009

Since this trend-watching strategy measures the previous 200 trading days, if the market is rising, the average will be smaller than the current market closing price. Your chart will plot the 200-day moving average (DMA) below today's market closing price. If the market declines, the moving average will turn southward, but the market will dip faster because the 200 DMA includes the previous "up" days. When the market declines rapidly, it will go from being above the 200-day moving average to below it. As it does so, the lines on your graph will cross as shown in Figure 18.4 (the same thing will happen in reverse when the market rises quickly).

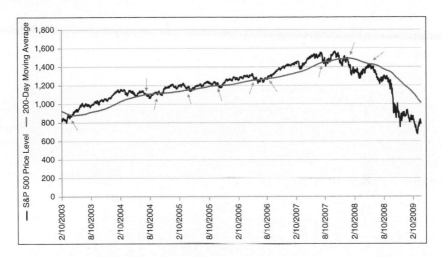

Figure 18.4 200 DMA Inflection Points

Any time the market gets above the 200 DMA, it's a bullish indicator. When it crosses underneath, it's a bearish one.

A Buy-and-Sell Signal: Jeremy Siegel's 1 Percent Band

If investors bought and sold every time the market crossed the 200-day moving average, they would have a tremendous number of transactions. When Siegel tested the 200 DMA in *Stocks for the Long Run*, he remedied this issue by creating a 1 percent band around the average. In other words, he theoretically bought when the Dow Jones closed by at least 1 percent above the 200-day moving average, and sold when it dipped 1 percent below.

Backed Up by History

By looking at several of the past decades, you can see these market trend indicators very clearly.

Let's first look at the Great Crash shown in Figure 18.5.

Figure 18.5   The Great Depression (1929–1932)

During this period, the market dropped an astounding 87.5 percent. Even an investor using the 200-day moving average would not have come out unscathed, but by using this trend-watching strategy with a 1 percent band, that investor would have lost 12.38 percent instead.* Nobody wants to lose 12 percent, but I would much prefer to lose 12 percent than 87 percent.

Now check out the 1970s shown in Figure 18.6.

And take a look at the first few years of this century illustrated in Figure 18.7.

---

*I'm using the S&P 500 in my calculations, along with Siegel's 1 percent band.

Figure 18.6   The Arab Oil Embargo (January 1973–December 1974)

Figure 18.7   The Tech Bubble (March 2000–October 2002)

In the chart in Figure 18.7, you can see that the sell signal would have come in late 2000. At that time, most people did not see a bear market coming. In fact, many analysts said it was just a dip that created a buying opportunity.

As you can see in Figure 18.8, in our last great bear market, the market went down 56.77 percent between October 9, 2007, and March 9, 2009. Someone using the 200-day moving average strategy with a 1 percent band would have lost 7.77 percent instead from peak to trough.

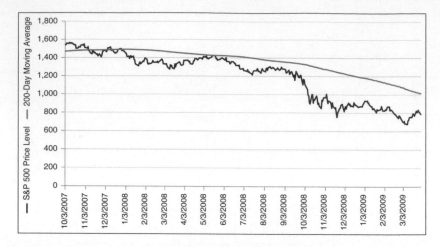

Figure 18.8   The Credit Crisis (October 2007–March 2009)

Returns and Risks

As you can see from Table 18.1, this strategy underperforms during some decades and outperforms in others. You can also see that by using the 200-day moving average strategy, your average return per year after trading costs would have been 9.05 percent. If you had bought and held over all that time, you would have made 9.49 percent. You would have

Table 18.1   The 200-Day Moving Average Strategy over the Decades

Decade	DMA Strategy (Net) Return	S&P 500 Index Total Return	DMA (Net) Return— S&P 500 Index	DMA Strategy Risk	S&P 500 Index Risk	DMA Risk/S&P 500 Index
30s	5.41%	0.20%	5.21%	20.52%	33.81%	60.69%
40s	5.28%	8.90%	−3.62%	9.59%	15.50%	61.85%
50s	16.24%	19.32%	−3.07%	9.80%	11.30%	86.72%
60s	7.31%	7.78%	−0.47%	6.11%	9.91%	61.64%
70s	4.99%	5.64%	−0.65%	7.94%	13.71%	57.96%
80s	18.12%	17.57%	0.55%	12.30%	17.12%	71.86%
90s	12.77%	17.84%	−5.08%	12.12%	14.06%	86.16%
2000s	2.27%	−1.31%	3.58%	10.67%	22.11%	48.27%
Averages	**9.05%**	**9.49%**	**−0.44%**	**11.13%**	**17.19%**	**64.76%**

given up an average of a third of a percent per year using the 200-day moving average strategy.

But remember, averages don't tell the whole story. If you had used the 200-day moving average strategy with a 1 percent band during the decade of 2000, you would have outperformed the market by a little over 3.5 percent per year, and taken just 48 percent of the risk. In the decades outlined in Table 18.1, you would have given up an average of a half of a percent per year, but taken *only 65 percent of the risk*. That's huge.

If you had bought and held during the Great Crash, you would have risked losing 87.5 percent. You could have lost up to 56.77 percent during the 2008 bear. If you lost those amounts of money while living on your investments you could go bankrupt.

Even Siegel, the author of the "Buy-Hold Bible," acknowledges the value of this less-risk strategy. "Although the returns from the timing strategy (the 200-day moving average strategy) often fall behind that of a buy-hold investor, the major gain from the timing strategy is that the timing investor is out of stocks before the bottom of every bear market . . ." he writes in *Stocks for the Long Run*. "This means that on a risk-adjusted basis, the return on the 200-day moving average is still impressive, even when transaction costs are included." Near the end of his chapter "Technical Analysis and Investing with the Trend," Siegel goes on to say, "The analysis in this chapter gives a cautious nod to these strategies, as long as transaction costs are not high."

A Buy Strategy

Critics of sell strategies argue that investors shouldn't sell because they won't know when to buy back. I have two responses to this argument:

1. The 200-day moving average strategy tells investors to buy when the market crosses above the moving average.
2. Buy-and-sell strategies are not mutually exclusive. Investors need to have sell strategies whether or not they have buy strategies in order to protect their principal. Protect your principal first, *then* worry about when to buy.

Using the 200-Day Moving Average

Investors use the bearish and bullish indicators provided by the 200-day moving average to decide when to buy and sell. But there can be periods where the market crosses the 200-day moving average so many times that it would be a nightmare to keep up with, not to mention the number of transaction costs you would incur—and the number of false alarms.

A false alarm occurs when an investor sells, the market goes back up again directly afterward, and the investor has to buy back in at a higher price. Some people call this "being whipsawed."

Obviously, no one wants to be whipsawed and no one wants to lose massive quantities of money. This is why many investors find a happy medium between the two by using a band like Siegel's (he used 1 percent above and below) in order to reduce the number of transactions.

Smart investors also use the close-of-business-day price to determine whether to buy or sell, and go into 90-day treasury bills during the time they are out of the market.

Why This Strategy Works

In general, people tend to become emotional about money. They over-react to financial news about the market, and sometimes react in ways that are counterproductive. The beauty of this kind of strategy is that it's mathematical. It removes emotion, and relieves investors from having to analyze the latest financial news. The reasons behind the stock market's rise or decline become irrelevant. Its purely mathematical equation provides investors with a predetermined trigger point that removes any uncertainty about how to proceed.

Why It Works Especially Well for Investors over 50

People who are over 50 need to protect their principal as much as possible. This strategy can do that.*

---

*Money Matters uses a proprietary metric, rather than Siegel's 1 percent band.

Yes, this approach can produce slightly lower returns, but the risk-adjusted return could actually be higher. In plain language, you only give up an average of less than half a percent per year, with a ton less risk. I know I've been beating the "protect your principal" drum throughout this entire book, but I'll say it one more time: If you an investor over 50, you are now on defense. You can't risk your retirement.

By removing emotions, significantly lowering your risk, and providing a floor underneath you (rather than the abyss), this strategy can give you peace of mind—as long as you have the discipline to apply it.

Chapter 19

The Trailing Stop-Loss Sell Strategy

Like the 200-day moving average (200 DMA) strategy, a stop-loss sell strategy takes the emotions out of trading by setting a predetermined sell point. But where the 200 DMA applies to the entire market, a stop-loss strategy is concerned with an individual investment. It helps you determine when to sell a specific stock, that is, when to "stop losses" on that investment.

When using a stop-loss, you decide upon a certain price that you do not want to go below, and create an order to sell the stock if it trades at that price. As an example, let's say you bought stock from Pretty Good Company (PGC) at $1.00 per share, and after a few considerations (which we'll talk about later in the chapter) you decided to set your stop-loss at 90 cents. If Pretty Good Company's stock price fell below 90 cents, your stop-loss order would be triggered, and that particular investment would be sold at the next available price.

The Trailing Stop-Loss

There are several versions of stop-loss strategies. I prefer the trailing stop-loss because it can help you to make a profit while protecting your investment.

The strategy is called a *trailing* stop-loss because the sell point rises along with (i.e., trails after) the stock price. If you bought Pretty Good Company's stock price at $1.00 and set your initial stop-loss at 90 cents, your stop-loss would be 10 percent. If you used the trailing stop-loss strategy and PGC's stock price rose to $1.10, your new stop-loss trigger point would be 99 cents, which is 10 percent less than $1.10, the new highest entry price. Your old stop-loss point becomes obsolete.

The trailing movement of the sell point can help you make a profit. It allows your stock to go up while protecting your gains. How? The exit point in the trailing stop-loss strategy only goes up. It never moves downward. By doing this, it helps you to limit your downside risk while keeping most of your profits. But, remember, this is a *sell* strategy. Once your stock dips below its trigger point, you have reached your risk tolerance level. You need to sell and preserve your money.

A heads up: Placing a sell order at 10 percent does not guarantee you will get out with only a 10 percent drop. Though the sell is triggered at 10 percent, the stock could drop further in the time it takes to fulfill the sale.

Setting Your Stop-Loss Point

How do you decide your exit point for a particular investment? By determining how much risk you want to take, and considering the nature of the particular stock you are dealing with.

As you know, I think investors over 50 should be cautious. It's incredibly important to carefully calculate your risk tolerance, remembering that if you're not living off your investments now, you soon will be. How much risk do you want to take with your standard of living?

Cautious investors who use the trailing stop-loss strategy tend to use tighter parameters, but they also need to take the particular stock's behavior into account.

Stock Behavior

Once you have figured out the amount of risk you're willing to take, look carefully at the stocks with which you'll employ a trailing stop-loss strategy. Each stock has a different amount of volatility, and you need to recognize and understand its typical behavior before determining an exit point.

For example, Pretty Good Company's stock might be really stable, and hardly move at all. Given its low volatility, you could put a 5 percent stop-loss on it. If that seemingly super stable stock dropped 5 percent, it could be a good indicator that there was trouble ahead and it would be a good time to sell.

But let's say you also have shares of Newfangled High-Flying Corporation. As the brightest, shiniest, most exciting company around, it might rise 5 percent every day for a week, then drop by 5 percent on the next Monday after the CEO says something silly on Twitter. It might rise 30 percent the next day when he apologizes by giving a bunch of money to charity. If you put the same 5 percent stop-loss you used for Pretty Good Company on the stock for Newfangled High-Flying Corporation, you would end up selling it when it was just behaving normally. Instead, you would probably want to put a larger stop-loss on that stock; say 15 percent. That way, if it rose 30 percent and then dropped 15 percent, you would still preserve a 15 percent gain.

Beta and Standard Deviation

How do you learn about the behavior of a particular stock? You can look at that stock's beta, and/or its standard deviation (see Tables 19.1 and 19.2).

A stock's beta tells you how volatile that investment is in comparison to the market as a whole. A beta of 1 means that the stock closely follows the swings of the market. A beta of less than 1 tells you that the stock is less volatile than the market, while a beta greater than 1 means that the stock's volatility exceeds that of the market. In other words, a stock with a beta of .90 would generally be 10 percent less volatile than the market, and a stock with a beta of 1.1 would be 10 percent more volatile. As you can see in Table 19.1, more stable investments (like shares in Pretty Good Company) will have typically lower betas than riskier (and sometimes more profitable) stocks like Newfangled High-Flying Corporation.

Table 19.1   Comparison of Betas of Some Famous Companies

Company	Beta
Aeropostale, Inc.	1.84
Buckle, Inc.	1.08
The Sherwin Williams Company	.59
General Mills, Inc.	.15
McDonalds Corporation	.28
American International Group	1.94
Genworth Financial	1.74
Principal Financial Group	1.86
Hershey Co.	.20
Walmart Stores	.45
Family Dollar Store	.39
Ford Motor Company	1.60
Prudential Financial	1.69
Metlife Inc.	1.87
The Coca-Cola Company	.48

https://www.google.com/finance.

Also known as historical volatility, the standard deviation calculates a stock's expected volatility in percentage terms by measuring the dispersion around an average. A high standard deviation indicates that the data points are spread out over a wide range of values; that is, the higher the percentage, the more volatile the stock (see Table 19.2).

Table 19.2   Comparison of Standard Deviation of Some
Famous Companies

Company	Standard Deviation
Aeropostale, Inc.	1.93
Buckle, Inc.	3.56
The Sherwin Williams Company	3.02
General Mills, Inc.	3.93
McDonalds Corporation	3.85
American International Group	3.98
Genworth Financial	2.69
Principal Financial Group	4.31
Hershey Co.	6.87
Walmart Stores	5.16
Family Dollar Store	5.89
Ford Motor Company	2.67
Prudential Financial	8.71
Metlife Inc.	3.33
The Coca-Cola Company	2.92

www.investorpoint.com.

Take Tech Stocks, for Example

Let's put aside our fictional examples, and see how the trailing stop-loss strategy could have worked with a real-life stock.

During the dot-com bubble, technology stocks rose very rapidly, but were also very volatile. For example, Qualcomm went up 6,000 percent between 1995 and 2000. It also jumped up and down, and up and down, over and over. If you had owned Qualcomm and understood the nature of that particular stock, you might have put a 20 percent trailing stop-loss on it. If you had, you would have stuck with Qualcomm through its normal volatility. You would have stayed with it as it rose 6000 percent, and when it turned, you would have sold. Yes, you would have lost 20 percent from its peak, but Qualcomm went down 85 percent. You would have saved yourself from that loss, and enjoyed most of that fantastic gain.

Remember, though, for a retired investor, the important part of this strategy is not making a profit, but *reducing the losses*. Like the 200-day moving average strategy, the trailing stop-loss strategy puts a theoretical floor underneath your investment. It can help you feel secure about investing without losing large amounts.

Chapter 20

When You Should *Not* Sell

D irectly after the tragedy on September 11, 2001, the market went down 20 percent.

Given everything we've talked about, if the market suddenly dropped 20 percent, your first impulse would be to sell and protect yourself, right? But there are times when you need to ignore your sell strategy.

Take a look at Figure 20.1, which shows what happened in the month after the 9/11 terrorist attacks.

The market rebounded very quickly. A month later, on October 11, 2001, the market was higher than it was on September 10. In just 30 days, the market had completely recovered from the initial shock caused by the tragedy on 9/11.

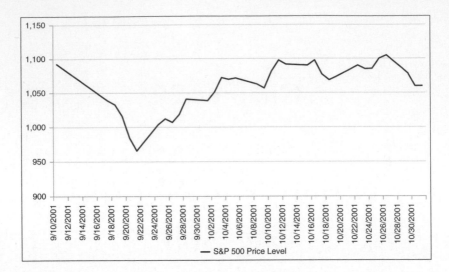

Figure 20.1   September 11 (September 10, 2001–October 31, 2001)

After September 11, everyone thought another terrorist attack was imminent. We had many meetings at our firm to discuss how to protect our clients if another attack did occur. In order to create the most effective plan, we had to consider a worst-case financial scenario: an event that would drive the United States' economy into recession.

We brainstormed: Could this happen? Could terrorists bring down the U.S. economy? What would it take? The destruction of an important harbor city might do it, we thought. It would be especially damaging if it were a harbor that handled most of the oil that came into the United States. That type of a shutdown could cause the economy to suffer so greatly that we could go into a recession and experience a bear market.

Little did we know that our worst-case scenario would happen, and that it wouldn't be caused by terrorists, but by nature. Hurricane Katrina destroyed oil rigs, devastated New Orleans, and basically shut down all the oil shipping headed into that harbor. But even our worst-case scenario didn't dampen the U.S. economy for long. The market bounced back within a month of the storm, recovering all of the losses it had experienced due to Katrina (see Figure 20.2).

The market's behavior after 9/11 and Hurricane Katrina reconfirmed that event-driven market drops tend to rebound.

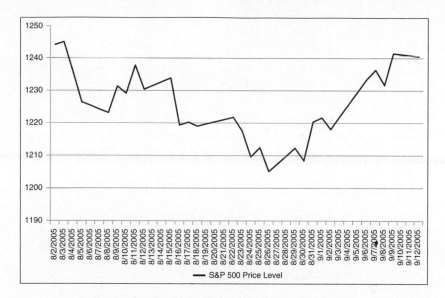

Figure 20.2 Hurricane Katrina (August 2005–September 2005)

More Event-Driven Market Drops

This event-driven market-drop phenomenon repeats itself over and over. The attack on Pearl Harbor precipitated the same kind of fall followed by a relatively quick rebound, as shown in Figure 20.3.

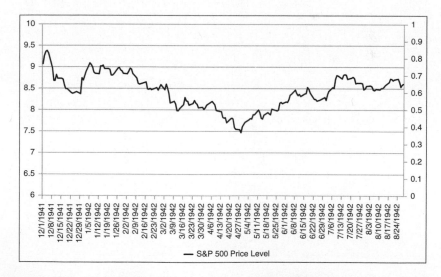

Figure 20.3 Pearl Harbor (December 1941–August 1942)

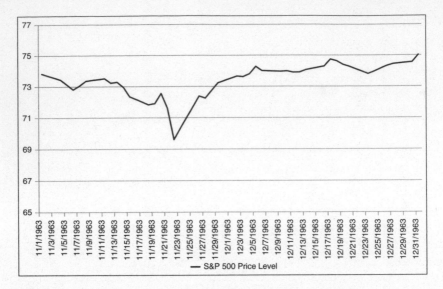

Figure 20.4   Assassination of John F. Kennedy (November 1963–December 1963)

So did Kennedy's assassination (shown in Figure 20.4).

Even the recent debt ceiling debate in 2011 caused the same type of drop (see Figure 20.5). After all, everyone was scared that America

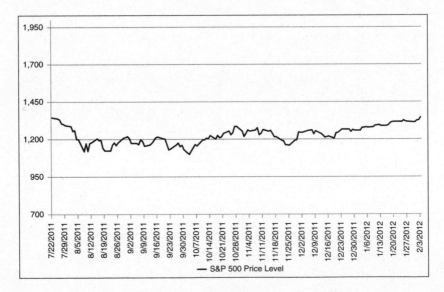

Figure 20.5   Debt Ceiling Debate (July 2011–February 2012)

was going to default on its loans and/or shut down the government. The market tanked during the debate that summer and went down until October, when it began to rise again. By January 2012, the market had come back.

Even though the market went down 19 percent while the debt ceiling debate was raging, it recovered quickly because the fall's trigger was a singular event. It wasn't a bunch of incidents or conditions that pointed to a weakening economy; it was the vote before Congress and the way that the situation had eroded Americans' confidence. It was a single event, and the market followed its historical pattern of rebounding after an event-driven drop.

> The four most dangerous words in investing are 'This time it's different.'
> —Sir John Templeton, investor/businessman/philanthropist

If You Can Point to a Specific Event . . .

You probably should ignore any drop, because it's likely that the market will rebound pretty quickly. In other words, if you can point to the event that caused the market to go down—if a bomb went off or a natural tragedy hit—you may not want to sell.

It's not easy to stay in the market during tumultuous times. The types of events that drive the market down are by nature unsettling. The period of time following such an incident can be very scary, and when you're surrounded by panicked people, all of your emotions and instincts will probably tell you to get out of the market *now*. Buy, hold, and sell will sound like a great idea—but for the wrong reasons.

It's not a good idea to sell in these kinds of circumstances because the market will probably rebound quickly. And, chances are, by the time you realize the market is reacting to an event, it's already gone down significantly. If you were to sell, you would have already lost a lot. To add insult to injury, you would be out of the market when it rebounded. You would have sold low.

If There's More Than One Reason for a Drop...

But...

- If you can't pinpoint a specific event...
- If a conglomeration of economic data tells you that the future looks grim...
- If it's looking like inflation, unemployment, and recession are coalescing to create a really ugly economic picture...

Pay attention.

In these circumstances, don't ignore the sell strategy you have designed to protect yourself. A market drop caused by an accumulation of many negative economic conditions is a big, red warning sign.

The 2008 Bear

Look at the lead-up to our last big bear. Though some people blamed the collapse of Lehman Brothers for the drop, this bear was not event-driven. You could see trouble coming from miles away.

The Dow Jones peaked at 14.093 on October 8, 2007. Over the next year:

- The unemployment rate went up dramatically.
- The real estate market began to collapse.
- The bond market tanked.
- The banking system was at risk.
- The United States looked like it was headed for a recession.

By the time Lehman Brothers filed for bankruptcy on September 15, 2008, the market had already gone down 22 percent.

As you can see in Figure 20.6, though Lehman's collapse may have been the nail in the proverbial coffin, it wasn't *the* event that precipitated the fall of the market.

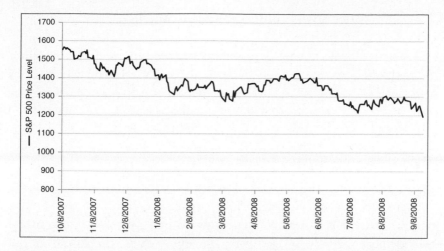

Figure 20.6   Pre-Lehman Collapse (October 8, 2007–September 15, 2008)

Since this was not an event-driven drop, the market did not rebound. In fact, Lehman's collapse poured fuel on the fire—not just a little gasoline, but an oil-tanker's worth. The market plummeted another 35 percent before it bottomed on March 2, 2009, for a total drop of 57 percent from peak to trough (see Figure 20.7).

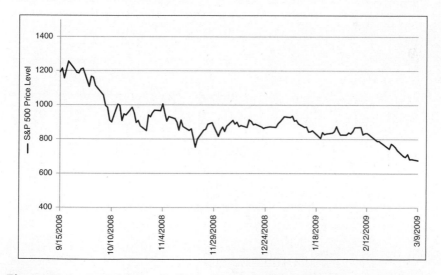

Figure 20.7   Post-Lehman Collapse (September 15, 2008–March 9, 2009)

Use Your Sell Strategy, Unless . . .

You designed a sell strategy to protect your investments, and you should use it. But as with any strategy, there are exceptions. Event-driven drops are those exceptions. If we have an incident that causes a sudden exogenous shock to the system, take a step back. Look at the recent economic data. Ask yourself if the event could push the economy into recession. And while doing so, remember that Katrina wasn't enough to derail our economy—an event that we considered a worst-case scenario did not drag the country down into a recession. Our economy is remarkably resilient. It takes a lot to change its direction. As scary as they can be, event-driven market drops do not typically lead to recessions or bear markets. In the vast majority of cases you should ignore them, override your sell triggers, and let things play out.

Chapter 21

Sell Strategy Pros
and Cons

S ell strategies are necessary, but they're not perfect. They can save you from enormous losses, but like any strategy, they have their pros and cons.

The previous chapter showed you one of the disadvantages. You can't just set up a sell strategy and forget all about it. You need to keep an eye on the market and the news, so that you can override your sell strategy if a drop is event driven.

False Alarms

Sell strategies can also produce "false alarms," that is, they will occasionally predict a bear market that does not happen. During a false alarm, the market goes down, crosses underneath its moving average, and triggers a sell. Then it bounces back quickly (an event-driven drop, perhaps), crosses above its moving average, and prompts a buy. When this occurs, you miss out on any gains you could have had from rising stocks because you sold before the rebound.

The reverse scenario can cost you, too. If the market rises quickly and triggers a buy, then drops enough that it goes below your sell point, your buy will be higher than your sell, and you will have lost money in that trade. You'll have been whipsawed.

I view those two disadvantages as small worries. If you make less than you might have, that's okay in my book because I believe the reason to use a sell strategy is to avoid massive losses in bear markets, especially ones like those that occurred in 1929, 1974, 2000, and 2008. I consider the fact that you don't perform as well when this happens as the insurance premium you pay to protect your principal against very large losses.

I believe it is also okay to lose money in a trade like I described above. There is no strategy that *never* loses. You have to consider the least of the evils: which strategy could cost you more? In the whipsaw transaction I described, your losses would not be as significant as they would be if you clung to buy-hold during a bear market.

My firm, Money Matters, had a false alarm in 2010. The financial environment was grim: The BP oil spill jeopardized the economy of the entire Gulf coast. Europe's economy was on the verge of collapse. The debt ceiling debate threatened to bankrupt America. If any one of those events had happened, we would have seen a full-blown bear market. The risk was enormous. We advised clients and the listeners of my radio show to get out of the market. As it turned out, none of those potential catastrophes occurred. The BP oil spill was manageable, the European crisis passed, the debt ceiling was raised, and all was well. Then the market rebounded and we missed the returns we could have made. Granted, that wasn't good. But the downside risk was so great that it was more important to protect principal than to worry about whether or not the sell was a false alarm. Investors avoided the bigger evil of a potentially life-changing loss.

The Financial Tornado Warning

On the flight back from a financial conference in 2009, I sat next to a young man from Oklahoma. When he asked me what I did for a living,

I told him I was a financial advisor. "Wow, 2008 must've been really rough for you," he said.

"It wasn't so bad," I replied, "because we advised our clients to be in cash for that entire year."

"How did you do that?"

"Well, we have what we call a 'sell strategy,' " I said. "We hit our trigger at the end of 2007, so at that time we advised our clients to sell all of their stocks."

Being from Oklahoma, he quickly related it to a danger he and his family face every year. "So it's like a tornado warning for your investments," he said.

I thought about it for a moment. "Yes, exactly. So tell me, what do you guys do in Oklahoma when you hear the tornado warning going off?"

"We go down into the storm shelter," he said.

"What happens if the tornado doesn't hit you?"

"I guess we had a nice game of cards."

"What do you do if the siren goes off a second time?" I asked.

"We go right back into the tornado shelter."

"And if the tornado misses you again?"

"Then I guess we played some more cards."

"How many false alarms would it take before you decided to ignore the alarm?" I asked.

"It doesn't matter how many false alarms there are," he answered. "I will take my family into the storm shelter every single time because I cannot afford to be wrong once."

It's the same with your sell strategy. Don't be afraid to take your money into the tornado shelter as many times as the siren sounds. While false alarms may reduce your returns, when that financial tornado does hit, you will be very glad you're sitting nice and safe in cash.

Transaction Costs and Taxes

Remember Jeremy Siegel's 1 percent band? He put an up-and-down tolerance around his 200-day moving average to help minimize transaction costs. A properly designed sell strategy will similarly limit the number of times you have to buy and sell, so transaction costs should not be significant. But even though you've minimized the costs, you may be tempted to hold on to an investment just because you don't want a transaction cost. Don't fall for that. If the situation becomes another 2008, you could lose 57 percent of your money just to avoid that cost. Not a good trade-off.

Taxes are a similar issue. No one likes to pay taxes, but they are a necessary evil. To be a successful investor, you will have to take profits when the time is right to sell. By doing so, you will create a taxable event. It's okay. You can't let the tax tail wag the investment dog. You have to keep your eye on your highest priority: protecting your principal.

Nobody ever lost money taking a profit.
—Bernard Baruch, financier/investor/philanthropist/statesman

A Cautionary Tale

A prospective client told me this story in 2002: "I bought Qualcomm in January 1998. I put $10,000 into it, and watched it go up. By December 1999 it had gone up 2,900 percent. My $10,000 was now $303,000!

"In 2000, Qualcomm started to go down. When it hit $260,000, I thought to myself, 'If I sell this now, I could pay off my mortgage and my car. I'd be debt-free and a long way toward retiring.' But I didn't sell. You know why? Because I didn't want to pay the taxes. I just didn't want to pay the capital gains taxes.

"So I rode it down. I finally panicked and sold my Qualcomm stock in January 2002, when it had dropped 73 percent from its peak. That $303,000 I had became $80,000.

"Normally, if you invest $10,000 and you sell it four years later for $80,000, you feel like you made a really good investment. But when I think that I had $303,000 and I didn't capture that, it makes me sick to my stomach."

Put the Odds in Your Favor

I hope you can learn from that poor guy. Don't put avoiding paying taxes ahead of taking care of your investments. Don't put anything ahead of preserving your principal. Instead, put the odds in your favor.

Las Vegas does it. The casinos know that somebody is going to walk in the door, plug a dollar into Big Bertha, and win $1 million. The casino will lose big on that lucky gambler. But they also know that a million not-so-lucky gamblers will lose way more than that to Big Bertha. The casinos have made sure the odds are in their favor.

I believe sell strategies are your best chance for not losing because, like the Vegas odds, they are based on mathematics. I have every confidence that the sell strategies I have outlined in this book should help protect you from bear markets in the future. The mathematical certainty gives me confidence, and it can put the odds in your favor.

Don't Be the Hare

Remember, I'm not talking about the odds of winning big. I'm talking about the odds of keeping the investments you need to live out your retirement years. Investors tend to be obsessed with maximizing returns and getting the highest possible returns at all times. To get these kinds of profits, investors often take more risk than is necessary.

If you are a prudent investor with a sell strategy, you will probably go through periods of time when you wish you were making more. You'll see that the market is doing better than your portfolio, and you'll wonder if you should be chasing some of those fabulous returns. You may have some regrets about your slow, steady course. Take solace. It *is* the right thing to do. When the next bear market comes along and blood is running in the streets, you'll be sitting comfortably in cash. Don't forget the fable of the tortoise and the hare. The hare was incredibly fast and very exciting, while the tortoise just plodded along, but who won the race in the long run?

> You are neither right nor wrong because the crowd disagrees
> with you. You are right because your data and reasoning are
> right.
>
> —Benjamin Graham, investor

Sell strategies help you avoid the worst-case scenario. Yes, they come with false alarms. They could cause you to underperform. They may cause you to lose money on the whipsaw. As I see it, those are much smaller costs than losing massive amounts of money in a bear market.

Chapter 22

More Reasons to Use a Sell Strategy

The best reason to use a sell strategy is to help protect your money during bad times. But just in case you're not 100 percent on board, let me give you a few more things to think about...

Bonus Reason #1 to Have a Sell Strategy

You Can Participate in Market Rises with Confidence

About a year ago, I was watching a very popular evening talk show when a guest asked the host how much money he had in the stock market. This host (we'll call him Mr. Talk Show) replied that he had just 20 percent of his wealth invested in the market.

"Really?" said the guest. "Isn't that kind of low?"

"Maybe," said Mr. Talk Show, "but I got killed in 2008. I don't want that to happen again."

On the face of it, Mr. Talk Show's decision to limit his exposure to the stock market seems eminently logical. Let's say he went from having 100 percent invested in the market down to 20 percent. If the market went down 57 percent like it did in 2008, he would only lose 11.4 percent. It would be bad, but it's not as catastrophic as what he went through in 2008.

But he's also missing out on 80 percent of the possible returns. In fact, at this writing, the market has gone up significantly since that particular show aired.

People reduce their exposure to the market because they lack confidence. They're afraid of losing massive quantities. But if they had a sell strategy, they would know that they'd sell at a certain point. They would protect their principal. They could invest more fully and participate in a rising market without worrying about huge losses.

The majority of us need to be in those rising markets. Mr. Talk Show can make a small interest rate on his millions of dollars and still be okay, but most of us would not make enough returns on 20 percent of our money. We cannot afford to have a tiny little portion in the market. We wouldn't be able to keep up with inflation, and it would eat our lunch. Which brings us to . . .

Bonus Reason #2 to Have a Sell Strategy

It Will Help You Keep Up with Inflation

In September 2013, we celebrated the fact that the market had reached new all-time highs. But they weren't really new high points in the market. Essentially, they were the same highs we saw in 2007, and earlier in 2000. In reality, in 2013 the market was just getting back to where it had been 13 years prior.

"Doesn't that prove the point that the market comes back?" you may ask. That's what the buy-holders would like you to believe, that the market has bounced back and that investors are back to even. But it's not true.

If we take into account the rise in the cost of goods and services due to inflation, there's no way that investors are back to even. When the Dow finally got back to 14,000, it had bounced back to where it was in 2000, but it did not have the same value. In fact, when you consider inflation, the Dow would have had to rise to about 21,000 to be at breakeven.

**"I found someone to speak to our associates
about inflation. His fee is $5,000...
$7,500...$10,000...$12,500...."**

SOURCE: Randy Glasbergen.

Real Life by the Numbers

As a financial advisor, I have to live in my client's world—the *real* world, where people have to continue buying food and gas and medicine. Just because the market "got back to even" does not mean that investors who rode the ups and downs of the market from 2000 until 2013 would be able to enjoy the same lifestyle they had prior to the bear markets. Why? A lifestyle that cost $60,000 per year in 2000 would cost $90,000 a year in 2013. If you lived on $60,000 a year in 2013, you would have to reduce your standard of living by 33 percent compared to where you were in 2000. A sell strategy can help you stay ahead of inflation by keeping you in the market during good times without worrying about the bad times.

Bonus Reason #3 to Have a Sell Strategy

You Can Feel Good about Using the Best Inflation Fighting Tool Available to You

As you can see, inflation is a dastardly, nefarious, inscrutable enemy that removes money from your bank account in terms of purchasing power.

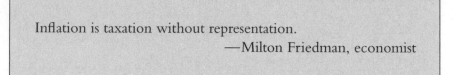

> Inflation is taxation without representation.
>   —Milton Friedman, economist

The stock market is the best inflation-fighting tool we have available to us. Stocks are better than gold. They are better than real estate. The stock market is the best inflation-fighting tool available to us, period (see Figure 22.1).

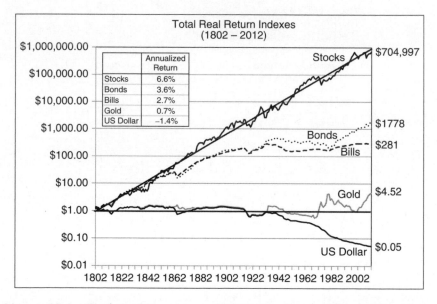

Figure 22.1 Total Real Returns on U.S. Stocks, Bonds, Bills, Gold, and the Dollar, 1802-2012

SOURCE: Jeremy J. Siegel, *Stocks for the Long Run 5/E: The Definitive Guide to Financial Market Returns & Long-Term Investment Strategies* (New York: McGraw-Hill, 2014).

Why does the stock market fight inflation so well? Inflation drives up everything. It's not just consumers who see prices rising; corporations also see increased costs. And remember, corporations need to keep their profit margins. Let's say a company decides it has to make 5 percent profit in order to be a viable business. If costs go up, in order for the company to still get that 5 percent margin, it has to raise prices. The profit margin stays the same, but the company sees higher dollar amounts. The after-inflation value is unchanged, but the dollar amount increased so it looks as though the company's profits went up.

If corporate profits are inflated, then their stock price will probably be inflated as well, since the stock prices are usually some multiple of earnings. This tends to cause a market rise in the initial phases of the inflationary cycle. For example, in the early 1980s, our country had the worst period of inflation since the civil war, and the stock market went up 49 percent, a fantastic rise. Inflation essentially inflated the stock market, too.

You can potentially benefit from the market's anticipated rise during the initial period of inflation. In fact, I think there is no better investment than the stock market during the early stages of the inflationary cycle. But even though the stock market is a fantastic inflation-fighting tool, it's also a double-edged sword. At some point, the market will peak and go down. In that inflated period during the early 1980s, the market didn't stay up. The weight of all that inflation was too much for the economy to bear. Consumers stopped spending, the economy went into a recession, and in 1981 and 1982 the stock market dropped like a stone. If you were still in the market, you would have suffered a loss and given back your gains.

The good news? A sell strategy can reduce or eliminate the harm you could suffer from the inevitable bear market, making you more inclined to use the stock market to fight inflation.

Chapter 23

The Magic
Number Strategy

Time to take action.

Before creating any action plan, you have to know two things:

1. Your current standing.
2. Your goal.

You wouldn't build a house without surveying the land. You wouldn't begin to build without knowing if you want a little cottage or a huge mansion. Creating a financial plan is no different. In this chapter, I'll show you how to figure out where you are financially, and what you'll need for the future.

How Strong Is Your House?

Imagine your portfolio as a house on the beach. If a hurricane approaches, you have to decide whether to leave or to stay. Your intuition can help you recognize the power of the storm, but you also need to consider the strength of your house. Fact: If you've got a little shack, you'd better not stick around. But if your house is strong enough to withstand the hurricane, you may be able to ride out the storm. How do you determine the strength of your financial house? You need to quantify how much damage you can withstand and still be okay. You need to know your "magic number."

Your Magic Number

Your magic number is the amount of money that you need in order to retire or to remain retired while sustaining your standard of living. In our firm, we use this number to form one of our sell strategies. It tells us the amount of money a client needs to protect. Your personal magic number can help safeguard your retirement investments, too. If the market is going down and your investments dwindle to the point where you're close to your magic number, you need to consider getting out of the market and protecting your principal.

Let's say that you have $2 million in investments and have determined that your magic number is $1 million. Though you certainly don't want to lose $1 million, you could afford to lose that much and still retain your lifestyle. You would still have your magic number of $1 million. On the other hand, if you have $1.2 million and a magic number of $1 million, losing $1 million and having to live on $200,000 would put you in deep doo-doo. You would need to get out of the game when you were down $200,000 in order to protect your magic number.

Knowing your magic number will help you to determine the point where you need to consider selling. Though this magic number does not qualify as a selling strategy per se, it can tell you when to become cautious. If you are at your magic number when all the headlines are shouting about the potential collapse of the financial system, or the potential recession, or the terrible unemployment numbers, it's time to get into cash. Having already decided the amount of money you can risk, you can now make an unemotional, pragmatic decision to protect your investments.

And once you've made that decision, don't let anyone convince you otherwise. Don't risk your magic number. If you stay in the market instead of getting out and protecting your investments, you may lose big. You may have to go back to work or reduce your standard of living. Can you do that? Can you find a good job after being out of the workforce for several years? Can you reduce your standard of living? You may be able to get rid of your mortgage by selling your house, but how long will that take? Any time you think about risking your magic number, take a good look at the potential consequences.

How Much Will You Need?

How much will you need for retirement? Every so often I'll read an article that says you'll only need 60 percent of your pre-retirement income. Really? You'll wake up the day after your retirement party to find that 40 percent of your expenses have disappeared?

Not one of my retired clients says their expenses dropped 40 percent. Sure, they no longer pay for lunch every day or gas for driving to work, but those are their only budget cuts. And now that they have leisure time, they're playing golf, traveling, and eating out—activities that cost more than lunch and gas. Their expenses actually went up, especially right after they retired.

You need to know how much you will need. Not a ballpark estimate, but a number as close to the actual amount as possible. Your magic number is that amount.

Calculating Your Magic Number

First of all, figure out your expenses (I've provided a handy worksheet in Table 23.1). Sit down and look at everything that you spend money

Table 23.1   Magic Number Worksheet: Part 1

Monthly Expenses during Retirement

Housing (mortgage payment, rent, property taxes, home insurance)	
Utilities, telephone, and Internet access	
Groceries and toiletries	
Prescription drugs and other out-of-pocket medical expenses	
Car payments and insurance	
Gasoline, car maintenance and repair	
Public transportation	
Health, life, and long-term-care insurance	
Clothing (include dry cleaning expenses)	
Restaurant meals and entertainment	
Vacations and travel	
Credit card and other loan interest (not including mortgage)	
Pet and veterinary expenses	
Cable or satellite TV	
Dining out	
Gym/fitness club	
Professional organization and club dues	
Subscriptions (magazine, Netflix, etc.)	
Hobbies and sports	
Lessons (music, art, etc.)	
Holidays and gifts	
Charitable donations	
Miscellaneous	
Total monthly expenses	

on each month, and I do mean everything. Your property taxes, your insurance premiums, your groceries, *everything*. Don't include income taxes and any money you're saving right now. Do include planned future expenses. If you plan to travel after retirement, build in a budget for traveling. Don't discriminate between needs and wants. If you'll spend money on something, add it to the list. Want to spoil your grandchildren? Add the amount you think you'll spend monthly. Do you contribute to charity or to your church? Make sure those expenses are on the list, too. Add all these numbers up and you'll have your total monthly expenses.

Now make a list of any sources of income that are not your liquid investments. Include pensions, real estate income, and Social Security. If you plan to work part-time after retirement, you can add that money to the list. Do you receive monetary gifts from family members? Include that, too. Make sure that you take the income and capital gains taxes out of these sources of income before you add them to the worksheet in Table 23.2.

Table 23.2 Magic Number Worksheet: Part 2

Monthly After-Tax Income during Retirement

Your pay	
Spouse's pay	
Your Social Security benefit	
Spouse's Social Security benefit	
Your pension income	
Spouse's pension income	
Miscellaneous income	
Total monthly after-tax income	

Now you know your total monthly expenses and your total monthly after-tax income. Subtract your expenses from your income. Your total monthly after-tax income minus your total monthly expenses will equal your monthly surplus or deficit.

If you have a surplus, great. That means that you actually may not need any investments to cover your cost of living. Your income sources can do the job all by themselves.

If you're like most people, you ended up with a deficit. You need investments to make up the difference between your readily available sources of income and your expenses. For example, if your expenses are $5,000 a month, and your after income tax income is $1,500 a month, you're short by $3,500 a month, or $42,000 a year. You need to make $42,000 a year, after taxes, from your investments in order for you to retire and/or retain your lifestyle.

To find your magic number, use the formula below:

$$\text{Monthly deficit} \times 25/(1 - \text{Your tax bracket}) = \text{Magic number}$$

Using my example, you'd multiply $42,000 by 25 and come up with $1,050,000. If you are in the 28 percent tax bracket, you would then divide $1,050,000 by .72 (1 − .28) and you would get a magic number of $1,460,000.

Why multiply by 25? That number represents 4 percent, a relatively safe amount to draw from your investments (I find it simpler to multiply by 25 than divide by .04, but either way works). Why divide by the after-tax rate? Because it determines the before-tax amount you need. You can only live on after-tax money and we need to incorporate the tax collector into the mix.

Remember, your magic number is the amount you want to protect. Any time your investments start to get close to that number, you need to be ready to get out of the market.

You'll want to recalculate your magic number from time to time as your income and expenses change. Finally paid off your mortgage? Your expenses will go down and your magic number will, too. Got hit with recurring medical expenses? If you don't have extra income to offset the expense, your magic number will go up.

If your investments are at or above your magic number, you should feel secure about retiring. If you're below that number, you have to do some soul-searching. You have four options:

1. Delay retirement
2. Plan to work part-time after retirement
3. Cut costs
4. All of the above

Weighing these options may not feel good now, but by understanding what you need and the risk you can take, you're helping to ensure that you will have the money you need in the future.

The Magic Number and the Musician

Your magic number is a marker that tells you when to protect your investments. It can also tell you when you have achieved your financial goals.

A few years ago, I met with a couple who had lost 90 percent of their money in the stock market crash of 2000. They had invested all their money in technology stocks and they lost big, big, big. At the beginning of that bear market, they had $2 million. By the end of it, they had just $200,000 left. As you can imagine, this loss had a big impact on them. The wife, who was the breadwinner, was in her 60s when the market crashed. She was now in her 70s and still working and adding to her 401(k) every month. The husband was a musician who didn't make a lot of money, but contributed whatever he could. Ten years after their loss, the couple had accumulated enough to achieve their magic number, having put away every penny they could.

"We've been scrimping and saving like crazy," said the husband, "We don't even take trips so we can keep saving."

"What kind of trips would you like to have taken?" I asked.

"I'm a musician, you know," he said. "I'd love to see the Grand Ol' Opry."

"How much would a trip to the Grand Ol' Opry cost?"

"Oh, about $1,400."

"Here's my advice . . ." I turned to the wife. "Since you've reached your magic number, you can stop funding your 401(k). Take that money, grab this husband of yours by the hand, and go to the Grand Ol' Opry. You've been through a heck of a stock market drop, you've paid your dues, and now it's time for you to enjoy your lives."

The husband looked like he was about to cry, he was so happy. The wife gave me a big hug.

"Yes, you have to save," I said, "And yes, it's important that you are disciplined. But you also have to have some fun. There's a balance there. Congratulations. It's time for you to enjoy."

Wouldn't it feel good to have that sort of confidence? To know that you could finally enjoy the retirement you worked so hard for all those years? I gave that advice because they had had reached their magic number. I knew that they could stop saving every penny they made. They could now start to spend some of it.

It's not guaranteed, but once you reach your magic number you can feel relatively secure financially—as long as you remember to protect it with a sell strategy.

Chapter 24

The
Rebalancing Strategy

Who's in charge, you or your investments?

You know not to believe in buy-hold. You understand the importance of a sell strategy. You know your magic number. But that's not quite enough. You need to be in charge of your investments—don't let your investments tell you what to do. You can't just make a bunch of investments, come back 10 years later, and expect something good to have happened. You need to be a proactive investor. You need to be the boss.

It's easier than you think to slide into reactive mode. Let's take an example shown in Figure 24.1: Let's say that you've analyzed your needs, done all the calculations, and decided that a 50/50 portfolio—50 percent stocks and 50 percent bonds—has the appropriate amount of risk for you. You've decided to invest $200, so you have $100 in stocks and $100 in bonds.

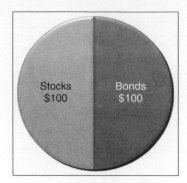

Figure 24.1   Invest $200 in a 50/50 portfolio.

You're cruising along and your stocks go up 60 percent. Holy cow! But your bonds lose 10 percent (Figure 24.2). Boo hiss.

You now have $160 in stocks and $90 in bonds. You made $50. That's 25 percent. Fantastic! This is great! Life is good!

But now you have a problem. Your portfolio morphed. It's not 50/50 anymore. It's now 64/36.

Your portfolio changed all by itself. You don't want that to happen. It's okay to be at 64/36 as long as it's your decision, but you don't want your portfolio deciding for you. Why not? Why not let the successes of your investments guide you? Because history shows that the investments

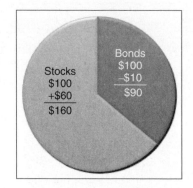

Figure 24.2 $200 Investment, now $250. Up 25%.

that go up the fastest are the ones most likely to go down next. Think about technology stocks. Remember how fast they went up? Remember how fast they came down? Or how about real estate? I know it sounds counterintuitive, but the investments that are doing the best are the ones that carry the most risk.

Not only is your portfolio now unbalanced, but 64 percent of your portfolio is invested in the risky assets, the ones now most likely to go down. Not very smart. You need to manage your investments. Don't allow them to decide how you should be allocated. Do you really want the majority of your investments to be in the stocks that rose so quickly? Remember that a decision not to sell is the same as a decision to buy. You didn't originally decide to buy that percentage of those stocks. You decided that your portfolio should be split 50/50 between stocks and bonds. You need to rebalance it to reflect that decision. Take charge.

Reap the Rewards of a Rebalanced Portfolio

Rebalancing your portfolio gives you several benefits.

Step Number 1: Rebalancing forces you to buy low and sell high.

You have to buy an asset from the slice of your portfolio pie that has gone down, and you have to sell an asset from the slice that went up (Figures 24.3 and 24.4). Mathematically, there is no escaping it.

Figure 24.3   Rebalance $250 Portfolio to 50/50

Figure 24.4   Rebalanced $250 Portfolio

Step Number 2: Rebalancing acts as both a buy and a sell strategy.

When rebalancing your portfolio, you sell investments. Rebalancing acts as a sell strategy by telling you what to sell and when. It also behaves like a buy strategy, letting you know when you needed more of certain assets.

Step Number 3: Rebalancing takes your emotions out of the equation.

Let's suppose I was your advisor. As in our example, we had decided on a 50/50 portfolio split. Then we had a gain on one side and a loss on the other. Your portfolio ended up at 64/36. Now we need to talk. I call you on the phone and say, "We need to rebalance your portfolio, so we're going to sell some of the assets that are making you 60 percent, and we're going to buy a bunch more of the investments that are losing you money." How would you respond to this particular phone call? Let me guess: "What? Are you nuts, Ken? I don't want to do that. In fact, I want to sell all of that 'minus-10 stuff' and put all of my money into the investments that are making me 60 percent!!"

This, of course, is not a good idea. You'd be taking much too much risk. But it's what your emotions would tell you to do. Emotions are not your friend when it comes to investing. They will lead you astray. Rebalancing provides you with a disciplined selling strategy and allows you to make investment decisions without being misled by your emotions.

Step Number 4: Rebalancing helps to control your risk in the long run.

Numerous studies have supported the fact that rebalancing mitigates risk. Even better, studies indicate the potential for increased returns. Anyone out there want to make more money with less risk?

Getting Off the *Titanic*

Less risk is the name of the game now that you're retired or retiring soon. By rebalancing your portfolio you are keeping yourself within the risk profile that you decided was appropriate for you. But sometimes a balanced portfolio may not be enough to save you from a bear market. What do you do when the market is eating all the slices of your portfolio pie? If all your investments are going down at the same time, you can rebalance all you want, but all you're doing is moving the deck chairs around on the *Titanic*. It might be better for you to get off the ship and into the lifeboat. When it comes to your investments, that lifeboat is called "Cash!"

You are in charge of getting out of the game. Don't let your investments lead the way. It's your retirement we're talking about. Take charge. Be proactive. Be the boss.

Chapter 25

Execute or Get Killed

I've just asked you to be the boss of your investments. Now I'm going to ask you to do something even harder: Be the boss of *you*. To successfully use a sell strategy, you must be disciplined enough to execute it. It's not easy.

If we surveyed 1,000 people and asked them, "What are the two things you need to do to lose weight?" every one of them would probably answer, "Exercise regularly and eat a healthy diet." The answer is very simple, but it's not easy. If it were easy, no one would be obese.

Your sell strategy is very simple, too. When you hit your trigger point, you sell.* You can't equivocate and think, "Well, this might resolve itself" or "It looks like the trend might change." If you second guess your plan or overanalyze the trend, you can get into trouble. By relying on emotions or trying to foresee the future, you may wait too long to act

---

*Unless a single event causes the market drop (see Chapter 21).

and lose a lot of money in the process. A sell strategy requires you to be dispassionate, and to act even when there is cognitive dissonance.

> Talent without discipline is like an octopus on roller skates. There's plenty of movement, but you never know if it's going to be forward, backwards, or sideways.
> —H. Jackson Brown, Jr., author

It Doesn't Matter Why You Sell...

Economist Robert Shiller famously called the years from 1995 to 2000 a period of "irrational exuberance." Turned out he was right, but in my opinion, it didn't matter. I don't care *why* the market goes up. As long as the market is rising, I want to be in it. I don't care if it is rising for irrational reasons, because it's making me money. I'm not going to fight it. On the other hand, if the market is going down, I want to be out of it.* I don't care what analysts say about the reason behind the drop. What's important is that I'm losing money. I don't care why.

It doesn't matter if you feel good or bad about the market. Once you hit your trigger point, it doesn't matter why you're selling.† You just do it.

You Can't Climb the Pyramids

It's not just emotions that can keep you from executing a sell strategy. Just plain life can cause you to neglect your strategy. It's too easy to make excuses: "I had that big meeting today" or "Market conditions are different this time" or even simply "It can wait."

You may not even be available to implement the strategy. What happens if you hear that the market is dropping like a stone when you're on a cruise and your tour of the pyramids is leaving in 10 minutes? You'll have to decide between finding a secure computer so you can execute the sell or climbing the pyramids. You'll probably climb the pyramids.

Inattentiveness is not a good strategy.

You have to have the discipline to act quickly, especially with the selling strategies described earlier in this book. If the market has reached your sell point you have to sell. You cannot delay. You cannot hem and haw. You cannot give it a little more time and see what happens. You have to act.

I'm not alone in warning you. In *Stocks for the Long Run*, at the end of the "Technical Analysis and Investing with the Trend" chapter, Jeremy Siegel said, "A final word: Technical analysis requires the full-time attention of the investor. In October 16, 1987, the Dow fell below its 200-day moving average at the very end of trading on the Friday before the crash. But if you failed to sell your stocks by that afternoon, you would have been swept downward by the 22 percent nightmare of Black Monday."

A Giant Bowl of Spaghetti

Not only does a sell plan require your full-time attention, your portfolio must be organized in such a way that you can take action quickly. You have to ask yourself, "If I had a sell strategy, could I actually implement it? If the market hit my sell point at the close of business today, could I sell everything tomorrow?"

For most of you, the answer is "no." You have a lot of moving parts to your portfolios. You have many different investments. You have accounts scattered here and there. You would have to go to seven different websites with five different investments in each account in order to sell all your investments. Your portfolio probably looks like a giant bowl of spaghetti.

Adopting the "buy, hold, and sell" way of investing can't be just a philosophical exercise. You have to reorganize your investments so that you can sell everything when the time comes. At Money Matters, that's the first thing we do with our clients. We properly diversify each portfolio to match the client's individual risk profile, and make sure we can sell the investments when the time comes. By cleaning up their portfolios, we get ready for the inevitable bear markets. We prepare to take action, unencumbered by a portfolio full of investments that could keep us from selling quickly.

> In theory there is no difference between theory and practice. In practice there is.
>
> —Yogi Berra, baseball manager

Remember New Orleans

Reorganizing and consolidating your portfolio will require some work on your part. If you believe you don't have the discipline or the organizational skills, don't use a sell strategy. You'll just prove the buy-hold argument right. The investors who wait too long to get out of the market and are slow to get back in don't make much money, and can lose a lot, just like the buy-holders claim.

A sell strategy can work, but the application of that strategy is as important (if not moreso) than the actual plan. Learn a lesson from the New Orleans tragedy. There were plenty of emergency response plans in place, but when Katrina hit, those plans were not executed properly.

The beauty of having a mathematical, fact-based sell strategy is that it gives you quantifiable data. Once you have that data, you can act on it. But here's the rub: You *must* act.

Chapter 26

A Simple Action Plan

Take action. Develop a financial plan. Use these five steps to help you protect your investments from the next bear market:

1. Ascertain your magic number so that you know how much money you absolutely have to protect. Include *all* of your expenses and sources of income when making your calculations.
2. Develop the portfolio allocation strategy that is appropriate for your situation, your objectives, and the amount of risk that you want to take. Make sure to consider taxes, inflation, and your spending habits before figuring out the rate of return you need to earn on your money.
3. Plan to regularly rebalance your portfolio over time. Controlling risk and maintaining the risk profile that is appropriate for you is always important.

4. Determine your sell strategy so as to protect yourself from the next bear market. Everyone's situation is different. You have a different risk profile, goal, and portfolio than your neighbor. The sell strategy that works best for you will be determined by those factors.

5. Implement your sell strategy when the time is right. If you don't feel that you have the discipline to implement your sell strategy, please seek out a financial advisor who believes in buy, hold, and sell. Remember, this plan is only as good as its execution.

Chapter 27

Armed with Knowledge

Buy-hold is an incomplete idea. You've suspected it all along. But now you have the knowledge to back up that hunch. Now you're armed with the information you need to stand firm in the face of buy-hold advice. You can debunk the myths with facts. You understand the importance of a properly designed and executed exit strategy. You have an action plan. You can feel more comfortable investing, knowing that you can buy, hold, and *sell*.

And now you can prepare, not only for your retirement, but for the inevitable bear market(s) that will occur. You can have a sell strategy. Like the Boy Scouts, you can "be prepared;" be ready for whatever might hurt you. You can make tough decisions dispassionately, because you have an exit plan in place.

Preparation can give you peace of mind. Think of a fire drill. It's designed to give you all of the information you need to survive. It then walks you through a scenario, so that if an emergency occurs, you can proceed to an exit without panic. A sell strategy does much the same thing to protect you from a "financial fire"—a bear market.

"I think my spell-checker is broken. It keeps changing l-u-c-k to p-r-e-p-a-r-a-t-i-o-n."

SOURCE: Randy Glasbergen.

I hope that in this book, I've made you aware that you will probably face several bear markets during your retirement. I hope that you decide to prepare for them, that you say, "This time I won't be fooled by the buy-hold myths. This time I will act. I'm going to protect my principal by creating and executing a sell strategy."

Maybe you were one of the lucky ones who sold and made it through the last bear market relatively unscathed without an exit plan. You may look back and say that you "saw it coming," but I believe if it wasn't a plan that kept you safe, it was luck. If you search your heart, I suspect you don't really know if you could replicate that, if you could "see it coming" again.

Luckily, you don't have to have a crystal ball. You just have to have a sell strategy to help you, and the fortitude to withstand bad buy-hold advice. I wrote this book with those ideas in mind, hoping that it would:

- Alert you to the dangers of the buy-hold myth.
- Give you the backbone and conviction to stand firm against the inevitable and popular buy-hold advice.
- Arm you with a counter philosophy.
- Help you to understand that, as a retiree, protecting your principal is more important than growth, so that you can be more comfortable erring on the conservative side of investing.
- Understand the importance of a sell strategy.
- Relieve any worry about outliving your investments by knowing there's a certain point you just won't go below.

More than all that, I hope that by arming you with the knowledge you need to protect your retirement, this book provides you with peace of mind, with a feeling of security in a world of volatility, risk, and economic unrest. I hope it gives you the chance to enjoy your retirement as you should—as a second childhood without parental supervision.

P.S.: What Do You Think Will Happen Next?

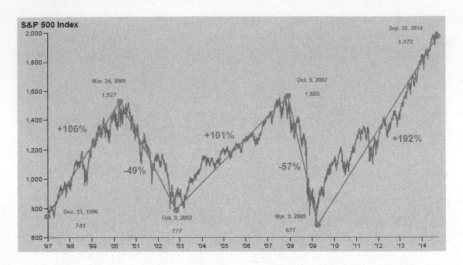

SOURCE: Standard & Poor's, First Call, Compustat, FactSet, J.P. Morgan Asset Management.

As you can see in the chart above, the market rose 106% leading into the dot–bomb bear market and then fell 49%. Then the market rose 101% and lost 57% in the credit crisis crash. Now the market is up 192%. What do you think will happen next? Don't you think it makes sense to protect yourself from the next bear market?

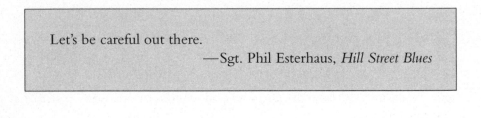

Let's be careful out there.

—Sgt. Phil Esterhaus, *Hill Street Blues*

Appendix

Diversified Allocations - Figures 13.2 and 13.3:

The hypothetical historical returns were created with the benefit of hindsight using the percentage allocations shown in the appendix. Simulated performance results do not reflect actual trading and have inherent limitations. Please see additional disclosures. Any changes will have an impact on the hypothetical historical performance results, which could be material. Hypothetical performance results have many inherent limitations and no representation is being made that any investor will, or is likely to achieve, performance similar to that shown. In fact, there are frequently sharp differences between hypothetical performance results and the actual results subsequently achieved. Portfolios are comprised of underlying indices.

Asset Classes	Benchmark	Definition	Diversified Portfolio
U.S. Large Cap	S&P 500	Standard & Poor's 500 Composite Index of 500 stocks, an unmanaged index of common stock prices. The Index is unmanaged and the figures for the Index do not include any deduction for fees, expenses, or taxes. It is not possible to invest directly in an unmanaged index.	55%
International	MSCI EAFE	A market capitalization-weighted composite of securities in 21 developed markets. The Index is unmanaged and the figures for the Index do not include any deduction for fees, expenses, or taxes. It is not possible to invest directly in an unmanaged index.	15%
U.S. Fixed Income	Barclays Aggregate Bond Index	Represents an unmanaged diversified portfolio of fixed-income securities, including U.S. Treasuries, investment-grade corporate bonds, and mortgage-backed and asset-backed securities. The Index figures do not reflect any deduction for fees, expenses, or taxes. It is not possible to invest directly in an unmanaged index.	30%

Disclosures

- All content is based upon investment strategies and financial planning methods utilized by Ken Moraif, Money Matters with Ken Moraif, and MMWKM Advisors, LLC. Direct and indirect references to market returns do not represent the performance of these entities or any of their advisory clients.
- MMWKM Advisors, LLC is the independent advisory firm created after Money Matters with Ken Moraif left Cambridge Investment Research. The persons who manage accounts at MMWKM

Advisors, LLC are the same investment advisor representatives with that responsibility at Money Matters with Ken Moraif. MMWKM Advisors, LLC accounts are being managed now using the same strategy as was utilized at Money Matters with Ken Moraif.

- Backtesting was used to test the validity of the advisor's exit strategy. Backtesting involves a hypothetical reconstruction, based on past market data, of how the strategy would have operated had it been used during a specified time frame. Returns do not show the impact of advisory fees and do not reflect actual trading in clients' accounts. Backtesting differs from actual performance, because it utilizes the retroactive application of a model that was designed with the benefit of hindsight. It is not indicative of the advisor's skill and does not reflect the impact that material economic and market factors might have placed on the advisor's decision making.

- Information presented is believed to be factual and up-to-date, but we do not guarantee its accuracy and it should not be regarded as a complete analysis of the subjects presented in this book. All expressions of opinion reflect the judgment of the author as of the date of publication and are subject to change. A professional advisor should be consulted before implementing any of the strategies suggested. Content should not be construed as an offer to buy or sell, or a solicitation of any offer to buy or sell the securities or services discussed in this book.

- MMWKM Advisors, LLC is registered as an investment advisor with the SEC and only transacts business in states where it is properly registered or is excluded or exempted from registration requirements. SEC registration does not constitute an endorsement of the firm by the Commission nor does it indicate that the advisor has attained a particular level of skill or ability.

- All investment strategies have the potential for profit or loss. Furthermore, having a sell strategy does not ensure that an investor's portfolio will be profitable.

- Past performance is not a guarantee of future investment success. Different types of investments involve varying degrees of risk, and there can be no assurance that any specific investment or strategy will be suitable or profitable for an investor's portfolio.

- Historical performance results for investment indexes and/or categories generally do not reflect the deduction of transaction and/or custodial charges or the deduction of an investment-management fee, the incurrence of which would have the effect of decreasing historical performance results.
- Economic factors, market conditions, contributions and withdrawals, and investment strategies will affect the performance of any portfolio. There are no assurances that a portfolio will match or outperform any particular benchmark.
- Asset allocation and diversification do not assure or guarantee better performance and cannot eliminate the risk of investment losses.
- Third-party ratings are no guarantee of future investment success. Working with a highly-rated advisor does not ensure that an investor will experience a higher level of performance. These ratings should not be construed as an endorsement of the advisor by any client. Generally, ratings are based on information prepared and submitted by the advisor.
- This manuscript was written with the assistance of a freelance writer.

About the Author

A Certified Financial Planner, Ken Moraif was recently named one of "America's Top 100 Independent Financial Advisors" by *Barron's*. His financial and retirement planning firm, Money Matters with Ken Moraif, was honored as one of the Top 300 Registered Investment Advisory Firms by the *Financial Times,* and is one of the top 50 fastest-growing financial advisory firms in the United States, according to *Financial Planning* magazine.

Ken's informative and entertaining weekly radio show, "Money Matters with Ken Moraif," is heard in many major cities. He is a frequent guest on CNBC and Fox Business and has written for or been quoted in *Forbes, Kiplinger's Personal Finance, MarketWatch*, the *Wall Street Journal*, and more.

Married since 1985, Ken and his lovely wife Fay have three beautiful daughters. A top-notch tennis player, Ken also finds time to ski, travel, and serve on the board of directors for the local Boys and Girls Club.

Index

Want to Learn More about How to Buy, Hold, and SELL?

I invite you to visit my website, moneymatters.net, where you can:

- **Sign up to receive my free email market alert**. If you're over 50 and want to stay on top of market news, subscribe today. We will never share your email address.
- **Schedule a free financial consultation with one of Money Matters, knowledgeable, friendly, and capable advisors.** Are you on the right road to your future financial goals? Our free, no-obligation review can help you determine:
  - Whether you are properly diversified
  - How to get income during your retirement
  - If you are at risk of losses in the next bear market
        At Money Matters, you'll get personalized service from expe-rienced professionals who'll meet with you one-on-one. You'll

get your own "watchdog" who will work hard to keep you up to date on the current market and keep your portfolio in shape.

When you come in for a complimentary visit, we will help you if we can. If we can't, we will tell you that too. Either way, there is no charge or obligation and we will part as friends.

- **Find a Money Matters seminar near you.** Our free financial seminars can help you:
  - Learn to combat the worst enemies of your financial well-being.
  - Select the retirement plan option that is right for you.
  - Plan your retirement income to preserve a comfortable standard of living.
  - Learn how to fight inflation with investments.
  - Find out how to diffuse the tax time bomb in your retirement plan.

These seminars are designed for people over 50 with a minimum of $100,000 of investable assets, not including real estate.

I want you to have the retirement you deserve!